The Ultimate Guide to Digital Marketing Agency

By

Megbo Beauty

Table of Contents

Introduction

Welcome to "The Ultimate Guide to Digital Marketing Agency" by Megbo Beauty. In this comprehensive guide, we will embark on a journey through the dynamic world of digital marketing agencies. Whether you're a seasoned digital marketer looking to start your agency or a business owner seeking to understand the role of digital marketing agencies, this guide is your go-to resource.

About This Guide

This guide has been meticulously crafted to provide you with a deep understanding of digital marketing agencies, their services, challenges, and opportunities. We will explore the intricacies of the digital marketing landscape and equip you with the knowledge and strategies required to thrive in this rapidly evolving industry.

Throughout the guide, you will find a wealth of information, including:

Insights into Digital Marketing: We will begin by demystifying the world of digital marketing and its significance in today's business landscape. You'll gain a clear understanding of why digital marketing has become an essential component of modern marketing strategies.

Types of Digital Marketing Services: Dive into the diverse array of digital marketing services, from search engine optimization (SEO) to social media marketing, email marketing, and beyond. Each chapter will provide a detailed exploration of these services and their impact on businesses.

Starting a Digital Marketing Agency: If you've ever dreamt of launching your digital marketing agency, Chapter 3 will guide you through the essential steps. From business planning and team building to pricing strategies and sales techniques, we've got you covered.

Client Acquisition and Retention: Discover effective strategies for identifying, attracting, and retaining clients. We'll explore the art of client onboarding, communication, and building long-lasting relationships.

Managing Digital Marketing Campaigns: Learn the nuts and bolts of managing successful digital marketing campaigns. From campaign planning to analytics and optimization, this chapter will provide you with practical insights for delivering results.

Measuring Success and ROI: Uncover the key performance indicators (KPIs) that matter most in digital marketing. We'll delve into data analytics tools, conversion tracking, and how to communicate success to clients.

Challenges and Pitfalls: Understand common mistakes and challenges faced by digital marketing agencies, along with strategies to overcome them.

Staying Current in a Dynamic Industry: In a rapidly evolving industry, staying up-to-date is crucial. We'll explore how to keep pace with industry trends, continuous learning, and the importance of networking.

Scaling Your Digital Marketing Agency: If you're looking to expand your agency's reach and impact, Chapter 9 will guide you through scaling strategies, hiring, and growth management.

Case Studies and Success Stories: Gain inspiration from

real-life examples and success stories of digital marketing campaigns and agencies that have left their mark.

Future of Digital Marketing Agencies: Finally, we'll peer into the crystal ball to discuss future trends and emerging technologies shaping the digital marketing agency landscape.

.

The Importance of Digital Marketing Agencies

In an era where online presence and digital visibility are paramount for businesses of all sizes, digital marketing agencies have emerged as invaluable partners. They bring expertise, creativity, and data-driven strategies to the table, helping businesses navigate the complex digital landscape and achieve their goals.

As we journey through this guide, you'll gain a profound appreciation for the role digital marketing agencies play in driving growth, brand recognition, and success for their clients. From optimizing websites for search engines to crafting engaging social media campaigns, these agencies are the architects of modern marketing success.

Join us in exploring the ever-evolving world of digital marketing agencies. By the end of this guide, you'll be equipped with the knowledge and insights needed to make informed decisions, whether you're considering starting your agency, collaborating with one, or simply seeking to stay informed about the digital marketing landscape.

Let's embark on this enlightening journey into the world of digital marketing agencies, where innovation, strategy, and creativity converge to create digital success stories.

Target Audience

"The Ultimate Guide to Digital Marketing Agency" is designed to cater to a diverse range of readers, each with their unique interests and objectives. Whether you fall into one of the following categories or simply have an interest in the world of digital marketing agencies, this guide is tailored to meet your needs:

.

Aspiring Entrepreneurs: If you have a vision of starting your digital marketing agency, this guide will provide you with a comprehensive roadmap. You'll learn about the essential steps, challenges, and strategies needed to establish and grow a successful agency.

.

.

Marketing Professionals: Seasoned marketing professionals seeking to expand their skill set and stay updated with the latest digital marketing trends will find valuable insights in these pages. Discover how to leverage digital marketing services for enhanced campaign performance.

Business Owners and Executives: Business leaders looking to understand the role of digital marketing agencies in achieving their marketing goals will gain a deeper appreciation for the services offered by these agencies. Learn how to select the right agency partner and maximize the return on your marketing investment.

Marketing Students and Educators: Students studying marketing and educators seeking resources to enhance their curriculum will find this guide a valuable addition to their learning materials. It provides real-world insights and practical knowledge about digital marketing agencies.

.

.

Marketing Enthusiasts: Anyone with a general interest in the world of digital marketing and a curiosity about how agencies operate will benefit from the insights shared in this guide. You'll gain a more profound understanding of the behind-the-scenes work that powers digital marketing campaigns.

How to Use This Guide

Navigating "The Ultimate Guide to Digital Marketing Agency" is designed to be user-friendly and flexible. Here's how you can make the most of this comprehensive resource:

Sequential Reading: Start from the beginning and progress through each chapter in order. This method is ideal for readers who want to build a foundational understanding of digital marketing agencies and their services.

Topic-Specific Exploration: If you're interested in a particular aspect of digital marketing or agency management, feel free to jump to the relevant chapter. Each chapter is self-contained, allowing you to focus on your area of interest.

Case Studies and Examples: Throughout the guide, you'll find real-world case studies and examples that illustrate key concepts and strategies. Take the time to analyze and reflect on these to gain practical insights.

Actionable Tips: Look out for actionable tips and recommendations highlighted throughout the guide. These are intended to provide you with practical steps you can implement in your agency or marketing efforts.

.

.

Interactive Learning: Consider using this guide in a group or educational setting. You can use the content as a basis for discussions, workshops, or assignments related to digital marketing and agency management.

.

.

Resource Reference: Utilize the "References for Further Reading" section at the end of the guide to explore additional materials and deepen your knowledge in specific areas.

.

Ultimately, "The Ultimate Guide to Digital Marketing Agency" is a versatile resource that can be tailored to your specific needs and objectives. Whether you're seeking to gain expertise, launch your agency, or simply understand the digital marketing landscape better, we invite you to embark on this educational journey with us.

Chapter One

Understanding Digital Marketing

Digital marketing has revolutionized the way businesses connect with their audience, promote their products or services, and achieve their goals. In this chapter, we will delve into the fundamentals of digital marketing, providing you with a clear understanding of what it is and why it matters.

1.1 What Is Digital Marketing?

Digital marketing encompasses a broad range of online strategies and tactics aimed at promoting businesses, products, or services through digital channels. Unlike traditional marketing, which relies heavily on print, broadcast, and physical media, digital marketing leverages the internet and electronic devices to reach target audiences.

Key Components of Digital Marketing:

- **Websites:** A well-designed website is often the central hub of digital marketing efforts. It serves as a destination where potential customers can learn more about a business and its offerings.

- **Search Engine Optimization (SEO):** SEO is the practice of optimizing web content to improve its visibility on search engine results pages (SERPs). High search engine rankings can drive organic (unpaid) traffic to a website.

- **Content Marketing:** Content marketing involves creating and distributing valuable, relevant content to attract and engage a target audience. Content can take various forms, including blog posts, videos, infographics, and more.

- **Social Media Marketing:** Businesses use social media platforms like Facebook, Instagram, Twitter, and LinkedIn to connect with their audience, share content, and build brand awareness.

Email Marketing: Email marketing involves sending targeted emails to a list of subscribers. It's a powerful tool for nurturing leads, promoting products, and maintaining customer relationships.

Pay-Per-Click (PPC) Advertising: PPC advertising allows businesses to display ads on search engines and other platforms. Advertisers pay a fee each time their ad is clicked, making it a cost-effective way to drive traffic.

Influencer Marketing: Brands collaborate with influencers—individuals with a significant online following—to promote their products or services to a larger audience.

Analytics and Data Analysis: Digital marketers rely on data to measure the success of campaigns, track user behavior, and make informed decisions about future strategies.

Why Digital Marketing Matters:

Digital marketing offers several advantages that make it indispensable for businesses in today's digital age:

Targeted Reach: With digital marketing, businesses can target specific demographics, interests, and behaviors, ensuring their messages reach the right people at the right time.

Cost-Effectiveness: Digital marketing often provides a higher return on investment (ROI) compared to traditional marketing methods. PPC advertising, for instance, allows businesses to allocate budgets more efficiently.

Real-Time Engagement: Digital marketing facilitates real-time interaction with customers through social media, chatbots, and email. This fosters engagement and builds trust.

Measurable Results: Digital marketing campaigns are highly trackable. Marketers can analyze data and adjust strategies on the fly to optimize performance.

.

Real-Life Example:

Consider a local bakery looking to increase its online visibility and customer base. By implementing a digital marketing strategy that includes social media marketing, content creation, and local SEO, the bakery can attract nearby customers searching for baked goods or cafe experiences online.

Case Study:

HubSpot, a leading inbound marketing and sales platform, has published numerous case studies showcasing how businesses have achieved success through digital marketing. For example, "How One Marketing Agency Improved Their ROI by 24% in Just 3 Months" highlights the impact of data-driven marketing strategies.

Understanding digital marketing is the first step toward harnessing its potential. In the following chapters, we'll explore various digital marketing channels and strategies in more detail, equipping you with the knowledge and skills to navigate this dynamic landscape effectively.

1.2 The Evolution of Marketing

Marketing, as a practice, has evolved significantly over the years, adapting to changes in technology, consumer behavior, and communication channels. Understanding this evolution provides valuable insights into the context in which digital marketing operates today.

Traditional Marketing: In the early days of commerce, marketing primarily took the form of word-of-mouth recommendations and simple signage. As businesses grew, print media, such as newspapers and flyers, became the primary means of reaching a wider audience.

Radio and Television Advertising: With the invention of the radio in the early 20th century, businesses gained a new medium for reaching consumers. Radio advertisements were followed by television advertising, which quickly became a dominant marketing channel.

The Internet Revolution: The internet's arrival in the late 20th century marked a pivotal moment in marketing. Businesses realized the potential of websites as digital storefronts, and email emerged as a new communication tool. Banner ads and pop-ups became common digital advertising methods.

Search Engines and SEO: As the internet expanded, search engines like Google emerged as gateways to online information. Search Engine Optimization (SEO) became crucial for businesses, as it determined their visibility in search engine results.

Social Media Era: The rise of social media platforms like Facebook, Twitter, and Instagram introduced a new era of digital marketing. Businesses could now engage with their audience on a personal level, share content, and build brand loyalty.

Mobile Marketing: The widespread adoption of smartphones enabled mobile marketing. Businesses optimized their websites for mobile devices, and mobile apps became a prominent marketing channel.

Content Marketing: The emphasis shifted from interruptive advertising to content marketing. High-quality, informative content became a means of attracting and retaining customers. Blogging, video marketing, and infographics gained popularity.

Data-Driven Marketing: With the increasing availability of data and analytics tools, marketers began to make data-driven decisions. Personalization, A/B testing, and targeted advertising became the norm.

Why Digital Marketing Matters

In today's interconnected world, digital marketing holds a central role in the success of businesses and organizations across industries. Here's why it matters:

1. Wider Reach: Digital marketing allows businesses to reach a global audience. Unlike traditional marketing that is limited by geographic boundaries, digital marketing can target customers worldwide.

2. Cost-Effective: Digital marketing is often more cost-effective than traditional advertising. For example, social media ads and email marketing can deliver impressive results with relatively small budgets.

3. Targeted Marketing: With digital marketing, businesses can precisely target their ideal customers based on demographics, interests, and behavior. This ensures that marketing efforts are directed toward those most likely to convert.

4. Real-Time Feedback: Digital marketing provides immediate feedback and data on campaign performance. Marketers can analyze metrics such as website traffic, conversion rates, and click-through rates in real time, allowing for quick adjustments and optimization.

5. Enhanced Engagement: Interactive content, social media interactions, and personalized messaging create more engaging experiences for customers. This engagement can lead to stronger brand loyalty and advocacy.

6. Measurable ROI: Unlike many traditional advertising methods, digital marketing efforts can be quantified with precision. Marketers can calculate return on investment (ROI) and assess the effectiveness of each campaign element.

Real-Life Task: Conduct a Digital Marketing Audit

To appreciate the relevance and impact of digital marketing, consider conducting a digital marketing audit for a business or organization. Here are the steps:

- **Evaluate the Current Digital Presence:** Review the organization's website, social media profiles, and email marketing efforts. Note strengths and areas for improvement.

- **Analyze Competitors:** Research the digital marketing strategies of key competitors. Identify what they are doing well and areas where your organization can differentiate itself.

- **Assess Data and Analytics:** If available, delve into the organization's digital marketing analytics. Look at key performance indicators (KPIs) such as website traffic, conversion rates, and social media engagement.

.

.

Identify Target Audiences: Understand the organization's target audience segments. Are they well-defined, and is content tailored to their needs and preferences?

.

.

Content Audit: Review the quality and relevance of the organization's content. Are there gaps in content that could be filled with valuable resources for the audience?

.

.

Mobile-Friendly Assessment: Check if the website and digital content are mobile-friendly. With the rise in mobile device usage, mobile optimization is essential.

.

.

Email Marketing Review: Analyze the organization's email marketing campaigns. Assess open rates, click-through rates, and email content effectiveness.

.

.

Paid Advertising: If applicable, evaluate the performance of paid advertising campaigns, such as Google Ads or social media ads.

.

By conducting a digital marketing audit, you'll gain practical insights into the significance of digital marketing for organizations. You'll also identify areas where improvements or adjustments can enhance overall marketing effectiveness.

In the subsequent chapters, we will explore specific digital marketing channels, strategies, and best practices to empower you in the dynamic world of digital marketing.

1.3 The Role of Digital Marketing Agencies

Digital marketing agencies play a pivotal role in the success of businesses across industries. Their expertise in navigating the complexities of the digital landscape, coupled with their strategic approach, can make a significant difference in achieving marketing goals. In this section, we'll delve into the multifaceted role of digital marketing agencies and how they contribute to the growth and success of their clients.

Core Functions of Digital Marketing Agencies:

Strategic Planning: Digital marketing agencies work closely with clients to define marketing objectives, target audiences, and key performance indicators (KPIs). They create comprehensive digital marketing strategies tailored to meet these objectives.

Content Creation: Content is at the heart of digital marketing. Agencies produce a wide range of content, including blog posts, articles, videos, infographics, and social media posts, to engage audiences and convey brand messages effectively.

Search Engine Optimization (SEO): Agencies optimize website content and structure to improve search engine rankings. This leads to increased organic (unpaid) traffic, enhanced visibility, and improved online presence.

Paid Advertising: Agencies manage paid advertising campaigns, such as pay-per-click (PPC) ads on search engines and social media platforms. They allocate budgets, create ad copy, and monitor campaign performance to maximize ROI.

Social Media Management: Agencies develop and execute social media strategies to build brand awareness, engage with audiences, and drive traffic to websites. They also monitor and respond to social media comments and inquiries.

Email Marketing: Agencies design, send, and analyze email marketing campaigns. These campaigns nurture leads, promote products or services, and maintain customer relationships.

Analytics and Data Analysis: Agencies leverage data analytics tools to measure the performance of digital marketing efforts. They analyze data to make informed decisions and continually optimize strategies.

Real-Life Task: Exploring the Role of a Digital Marketing Agency

To gain a deeper understanding of the role of a digital marketing agency, consider the following real-life task:

Task: Conduct an Interview or Research a Digital Marketing Agency

Select a Digital Marketing Agency: Choose a digital marketing agency in your area or within your industry that piques your interest. You can find agencies through online searches, social media, or referrals.

.

.

Contact the Agency: Reach out to the agency to inquire about the possibility of conducting an interview or gathering information about their services. Many agencies are open to sharing insights into their work.

.

.

Prepare Questions: If you secure an interview or consultation with the agency, prepare a list of questions to ask. These questions may include:

.

- How do you approach developing digital marketing strategies for your clients?
- Can you provide examples of successful campaigns you've managed for clients?
- What tools and technologies do you use for analytics and reporting?
- How do you stay updated with the latest digital marketing trends and algorithm changes?

What do you consider the most significant challenges and opportunities in digital marketing today?

.

Conduct the Interview or Research: During the interview or research, gather information about the agency's client success stories, the strategies they employ, and their approach to delivering results.

.

.

Analyze and Reflect: After the interview or research, analyze the insights you've gathered. Consider how the agency's role aligns with the core functions mentioned earlier and how their services contribute to the success of their clients.

.

This task will provide you with practical insights into how a digital marketing agency operates and the value it brings to businesses. You'll gain a firsthand perspective on the strategies and techniques that agencies employ to navigate the digital landscape and drive success for their clients.

In the subsequent chapters, we'll explore digital marketing channels and strategies in more depth, offering you a comprehensive understanding of how agencies leverage these tools to achieve marketing objectives

Chapter Two

Types of Digital Marketing Services

In this chapter, we will dive into various types of digital marketing services offered by agencies, starting with one of the foundational pillars of online visibility and organic traffic growth: Search Engine Optimization (SEO).

2.1 Search Engine Optimization (SEO)

Search Engine Optimization, or SEO, is the practice of optimizing digital content, websites, and online assets to rank higher on search engine results pages (SERPs). The goal is to increase organic (unpaid) visibility and attract targeted traffic from search engines like Google, Bing, and Yahoo.

Key Elements of SEO:

.

On-Page SEO: This involves optimizing individual web pages to improve their search engine rankings. Key on-page elements include optimizing content with relevant keywords, meta tags, and ensuring proper HTML structure.

.

.

Off-Page SEO: Off-page SEO focuses on improving a website's authority and reputation through external factors. This includes link-building strategies, social media signals, and mentions on authoritative websites.

.

.

Technical SEO: Technical SEO ensures that a website's structure and backend components are search-engine-friendly. This includes optimizing site speed, mobile-friendliness, and XML sitemaps.

.

.

Local SEO: Local SEO targets location-specific searches, making it crucial for businesses with physical locations. It includes optimizing Google My Business profiles, local citations, and customer reviews.

.

Why SEO Matters:

SEO is a cornerstone of digital marketing for several reasons:

.

Increased Organic Traffic: By optimizing for relevant keywords and providing valuable content, businesses can attract users actively searching for their products or services.

Cost-Effective: Organic search traffic is free, making SEO a cost-effective way to drive visitors to a website.

Credibility and Trust: High search engine rankings are often associated with trustworthiness and authority in a given industry.

Competitive Advantage: Outranking competitors in search results can lead to increased market share and brand visibility.

.

Real-Life Success Story:

Case Study: Moz

Moz, a well-known SEO software company, regularly publishes case studies showcasing the impact of SEO on various businesses. One such case study, "How We Ranked #1 for a High-Volume Keyword in Under 3 Months," details how Moz's own SEO efforts led to top rankings and significant traffic growth.

Real-Life Task: Conduct an SEO Audit

To appreciate the significance of SEO and gain practical

experience, consider conducting an SEO audit for a website, whether it's your own or one you're familiar with. Here's how:

Task: Perform an SEO Audit

.

Select a Website: Choose a website to audit. It could be your own if you have one, or you can select a website of interest. Ensure the website has a variety of pages to analyze.

.

.

Use SEO Tools: Utilize SEO tools such as Google's PageSpeed Insights, Moz's Site Crawl, or SEMrush's Site Audit to evaluate various aspects of SEO. Focus on areas like page load speed, meta tags, keyword usage, and backlinks.

.

.

Keyword Analysis: Analyze the website's keyword strategy. Are relevant keywords integrated into content, meta titles, and descriptions? Are there opportunities to target additional keywords?

.

.

Content Evaluation: Review the quality and relevance of the website's content. Identify areas where content can be improved or expanded to provide more value to users.

.

.

Backlink Analysis: If possible, assess the website's backlink profile. Are there opportunities to acquire high-quality backlinks from authoritative sources?

.

.

Technical Assessment: Evaluate technical aspects such as site speed, mobile-friendliness, and URL structure. Identify any technical issues that may hinder SEO performance.

.

.

Recommendations: Based on your analysis, compile a list of recommendations for improving the website's SEO. Prioritize these recommendations to provide a clear action plan.

.

By conducting an SEO audit, you'll gain hands-on experience in assessing a website's SEO health and identifying opportunities for improvement. This practical exercise will deepen your understanding of SEO's importance and how it contributes to a website's visibility and success.

In the upcoming chapters, we will explore additional digital marketing services and strategies that digital marketing agencies employ to help businesses achieve their goals in the ever-evolving digital landscape.

Types of Digital Marketing Services

Continuing our exploration of digital marketing services, let's delve into two powerful strategies: Pay-Per-Click (PPC) Advertising and Content Marketing.

2.2 Pay-Per-Click (PPC) Advertising

Pay-Per-Click (PPC) advertising is a model where advertisers pay a fee each time their ad is clicked. It's a way to buy visits to your website rather than attempting to "earn" those visits organically through SEO. Here's how it works:

Key Elements of PPC Advertising:

Keyword Research: Identifying the right keywords to target is crucial. This involves researching keywords that potential customers are likely to use when searching for products or services.

Ad Copy: Crafting compelling ad copy that resonates with the target audience is essential. Ads should provide a clear call-to-action and align with the user's search intent.

Bid Management: Managing bids effectively to ensure that ads appear in prominent positions without overspending is a key part of PPC management.

Quality Score: Search engines like Google assess the quality of ads and landing pages. A higher quality score can lead to lower costs and better ad positions.

Ad Extensions: Using ad extensions like site links, callouts, and structured snippets can enhance ad visibility and provide additional information to users.

Why PPC Advertising Matters:

Immediate Results: Unlike organic search efforts, PPC advertising can generate instant results. Ads appear as soon as the campaign is live.

Targeted Advertising: Advertisers can precisely target specific demographics, locations, and user behaviors, ensuring that ads reach the right audience.

Control Over Budget: Advertisers have full control over their budget, allowing them to set daily or monthly limits.

Measurable ROI: PPC advertising offers detailed tracking and analytics, enabling advertisers to measure the ROI of each campaign accurately.

.

Real-Life Success Story:

Case Study: WordStream

WordStream, a digital advertising software company, regularly publishes case studies highlighting the success stories of their clients. For instance, the case study "How One SaaS Company Used Google Ads to Achieve a 14X ROAS" showcases the impact of PPC advertising on a software company's return on ad spend (ROAS).

Real-Life Task: Create a Mock PPC Campaign

To gain practical experience with PPC advertising, consider creating a mock PPC campaign for a fictional product or service. Follow these steps:

Task: Create a Mock PPC Campaign

.

Choose a Product/Service: Select a fictional product or service to promote. Define its unique selling points and target audience.

.

.

Keyword Research: Perform keyword research to identify relevant keywords for your campaign. Use tools like Google's

Keyword Planner.

·

·

Craft Ad Copy: Write ad copy that aligns with your chosen keywords and speaks to your target audience's needs and interests.

·

·

Set Up a Mock Campaign: If you have access to a PPC platform like Google Ads, set up a mock campaign. Otherwise, you can create a spreadsheet outlining your campaign structure, keywords, ad groups, and budgets.

·

·

Monitor and Optimize: If you've set up a live campaign, monitor its performance daily. Adjust bids, test different ad variations, and analyze the results.

·

·

Report and Reflect: Create a report summarizing the performance of your mock campaign. Reflect on what worked well and what could be improved.

·

This task allows you to experience the process of planning, creating, and managing a PPC campaign, providing valuable insights into the intricacies of paid advertising.

2.3 Content Marketing

Content marketing involves creating and distributing valuable, relevant content to attract and engage a target audience. This approach focuses on providing information and resources that resonate with potential customers. Here's why content marketing matters:

.

Building Authority: High-quality content establishes your brand as an authority in your industry.

Audience Engagement: Valuable content engages your audience and fosters trust and loyalty.

SEO Benefits: Content creation, when optimized, can improve SEO and drive organic traffic.

Lead Generation: Content can act as a lead generation tool, capturing contact information from interested users.

Education and Value: Content marketing educates your audience, providing them with the information they need to make informed decisions.

.

Real-Life Success Story:

Case Study: HubSpot

HubSpot, a leader in inbound marketing and sales software, has an extensive collection of case studies that illustrate the power of content marketing. One case study, "How I Grew My Declining Traffic by 44% (In An Industry Riddled with Decline)," showcases how a HubSpot customer leveraged content marketing to reverse declining website traffic.

Real-Life Task: Create a Content Calendar

To gain practical experience in content marketing, create a content calendar for a fictional business or blog. Follow these steps:

Task: Create a Content Calendar

Define the Audience: Identify your target audience and their needs or interests.

Content Goals: Determine the goals of your content marketing efforts. Is it brand awareness, lead generation, or customer education?

Topic Research: Research topics that resonate with your audience. Use tools like Google Trends or keyword research tools to find popular and relevant topics.

Content Types: Decide on the types of content you'll create, such as blog posts, videos, infographics, or podcasts.

Create a Calendar: Create a calendar outlining your content schedule. Specify publication dates, content titles, and the responsible team members.

Promotion Plan: Outline how you'll promote your content. Consider using social media, email marketing, or outreach to industry influencers.

Measurement: Define key performance indicators (KPIs) to measure the success of your content. These could include page views, social shares, or lead conversions.

By creating a content calendar and planning content marketing efforts, you'll gain hands-on experience in content strategy and execution. This exercise will prepare you to leverage content marketing effectively for businesses or organizations.

In the upcoming chapters, we will explore additional digital marketing services and strategies employed by digital marketing agencies to help businesses thrive in the digital landscape.

2.4 Social Media Marketing

Social Media Marketing involves using social media platforms to connect with your audience, build your brand, increase sales, and drive website traffic. It encompasses a range of activities, from creating and sharing content to engaging with followers and running paid advertising campaigns.

Key Elements of Social Media Marketing:

- **Content Creation:** Social media marketers create and curate content that resonates with their target audience. This content can include text, images, videos, infographics, and more.

- **Audience Engagement:** Engagement is crucial on social media. Responding to comments, messages, and mentions helps build relationships with followers.

- **Social Advertising:** Paid social media advertising allows marketers to target specific demographics, interests, and behaviors. It's an effective way to reach a broader audience.

Analytics and Monitoring: Social media marketers use analytics tools to track the performance of their campaigns. They measure metrics like reach, engagement, click-through rates, and conversions.

Why Social Media Marketing Matters:

Audience Reach: Social media platforms have billions of active users, making them an ideal place to connect with your target audience.

Brand Building: Consistent social media presence can build brand recognition and loyalty.

Customer Feedback: Social media allows for real-time feedback and interaction with customers.

Cost-Effective: Organic social media efforts are cost-effective, and paid advertising can be budget-friendly with precise targeting.

Real-Life Success Story:

Case Study: Wendy's

Wendy's, the fast-food chain, is known for its witty and humorous social media presence. Their Twitter account, in particular, gained attention for its clever and engaging responses to customer inquiries and comments. This approach led to increased brand visibility and a dedicated following.

Real-Life Task: Create a Social Media Content Calendar

To gain practical experience in social media marketing, create a social media content calendar for a fictional business or organization. Follow these steps:

Task: Create a Social Media Content Calendar

.

Choose a Business: Select a fictional business or organization to represent.

.

Define Objectives: Determine the social media marketing objectives for your chosen business. Is it brand awareness, engagement, lead generation, or something else?

.

Select Platforms: Identify the social media platforms that align with your business and target audience. Consider platforms like Facebook, Instagram, Twitter, LinkedIn, or others.

.

Content Themes: Decide on the themes and topics for your social media content. These should align with your objectives and resonate with your audience.

.

Create a Calendar: Build a content calendar that outlines what you'll post on each platform and when. Include details like post copy, images or graphics, and relevant hashtags.

.

Engagement Plan: Outline how you'll engage with your audience. This includes responding to comments, initiating conversations, and addressing customer inquiries or feedback.

.

Measurement: Define key performance indicators (KPIs) to track the success of your social media efforts. These may include likes, shares, comments, clicks, or conversions.

By creating a social media content calendar, you'll develop practical skills in social media strategy, content planning, and audience engagement. This exercise will prepare you to excel in social media marketing.

2.5 Email Marketing

Email Marketing remains one of the most effective digital marketing channels for building and nurturing customer relationships. It involves sending targeted emails to a list of subscribers with the goal of achieving specific business objectives.

Key Elements of Email Marketing:

List Building: Building and maintaining a quality email list is essential. This can be done through website sign-up forms, lead magnets, and other opt-in methods.

Segmentation: Segmenting your email list allows you to send tailored content to specific groups based on their interests, behaviors, or demographics.

Email Content: Creating compelling and relevant email content is crucial. This includes crafting subject lines, body copy, images, and calls to action (CTAs).

Automation: Email automation allows you to send personalized emails triggered by specific actions or behaviors. For example, a welcome series for new subscribers.

Testing and Optimization: Email marketers often A/B test various elements to optimize campaigns for better open rates, click-through rates, and conversions.

Why Email Marketing Matters:

Direct Communication: Email provides a direct line of communication to your audience, making it a powerful tool for personalized engagement.

Conversion Rates: Email marketing consistently delivers high conversion rates, making it effective for sales and lead nurturing.

Cost-Effective: Compared to many other marketing channels, email marketing is cost-effective, with a strong ROI.

Data and Analytics: Email platforms offer robust analytics, allowing marketers to measure the success of campaigns and make data-driven decisions.

Real-Life Success Story:

Case Study: Airbnb

Airbnb, the online marketplace for lodging and travel experiences, has mastered email marketing. They send personalized, well-timed emails to users, providing them with relevant travel recommendations, updates on bookings, and special offers. This approach has contributed to user retention and brand loyalty.

Real-Life Task: Create an Email Marketing Campaign

To gain practical experience in email marketing, create a mock email marketing campaign for a fictional business or organization. Here's how:

Task: Create an Email Marketing Campaign

.

Choose a Business: Select a fictional business or organization to represent.

.

.

Define Campaign Goals: Determine the objectives for your email marketing campaign. Is it to promote a product, nurture leads, or re-engage inactive subscribers?

.

.

Segment Your List: If you have a fictional email list, segment it based on criteria relevant to your campaign goals.

.

.

Create Email Content: Craft compelling email content that aligns with your campaign objectives. Consider the subject line, body copy, images, and CTAs.

.

.

Design the Email: Use an email marketing platform or design software to create visually appealing emails. Ensure they are mobile-responsive.

.

.

Set Up Automation: If applicable, set up automation triggers for your campaign. For example, a welcome email series for new subscribers.

.

.

Send and Monitor: Send your campaign to your fictional email list and monitor its performance. Track open rates, click-through rates, and conversions.

.

.

Analysis and Reflection: After the campaign, analyze the results and reflect on what worked well and what could be improved.

.

Creating a mock email marketing campaign will provide hands-on experience in email marketing strategy, content creation, and campaign analysis. This exercise will equip you with the skills to effectively leverage email marketing for real-world scenarios.

In the subsequent chapters, we will explore additional digital marketing services and strategies employed by digital marketing agencies to help businesses succeed in the dynamic digital landscape.
Continuing our exploration of digital marketing services, we will now delve into two influential strategies: Influencer Marketing and Affiliate Marketing.

2.6 Influencer Marketing

Influencer Marketing is a strategy that involves collaborating with individuals who have a significant and engaged following on social media or other digital platforms. These influencers can promote products, services, or brands to their loyal audience. Here's how it works:

Key Elements of Influencer Marketing:

- **Influencer Selection:** Finding the right influencers is crucial. Factors like niche relevance, audience size, engagement rate, and authenticity are considered.

- **Campaign Planning:** Brands and influencers collaborate on campaign objectives, content creation, and messaging.

- **Content Creation:** Influencers produce content that showcases the brand's product or service. This content can take various forms, such as Instagram posts, YouTube videos, or blog reviews.

- **Audience Engagement:** Influencers engage with their audience through comments, likes, and shares, fostering trust and interaction.

- **Measurement:** Key performance indicators (KPIs) like reach, engagement, click-through rates, and conversions are used to evaluate campaign success.

Why Influencer Marketing Matters:

-

Trust and Authenticity: Influencers have built trust with their audience, making their recommendations more credible.

Extended Reach: Collaborating with influencers allows brands to tap into the influencer's established audience.

Targeted Marketing: Influencers often have niche-specific followers, ensuring that campaigns reach the right demographics.

Content Variety: Influencer-generated content adds diversity to a brand's marketing materials.

-

Real-Life Success Story:

Case Study: Daniel Wellington

The watch brand Daniel Wellington achieved remarkable success through influencer marketing. They collaborated with micro-influencers on Instagram, who posted stylized images featuring Daniel Wellington watches. This strategy helped the brand quickly gain recognition and credibility, resulting in significant sales growth.

Real-Life Task: Develop an Influencer Marketing Campaign

To gain practical experience in influencer marketing, create a mock influencer marketing campaign for a fictional product or brand. Follow these steps:

Task: Develop an Influencer Marketing Campaign

-

Select a Product/Brand: Choose a fictional product or brand to promote through influencer marketing.

.

.

Identify Target Audience: Define the target audience for your product or brand. This will guide your influencer selection.

.

.

Influencer Research: Research and identify fictional influencers who align with your product or brand's niche and target audience.

.

.

Campaign Objectives: Determine the objectives of your campaign. Are you aiming for brand awareness, increased sales, or something else?

.

.

Influencer Outreach: Create a proposal to reach out to your selected fictional influencers. Outline the campaign details, compensation (even if it's fictional), and expectations.

.

.

Content Collaboration: Collaborate with influencers on the creation of content that promotes your product or brand. Ensure it aligns with their style and resonates with their audience.

.

.

Monitoring and Reporting: Track the performance of the influencer marketing campaign, monitoring metrics like engagement and conversions.

.

Analysis and Reflection: After the campaign, analyze the results and reflect on what worked well and what could be improved.

By developing a mock influencer marketing campaign, you'll gain hands-on experience in influencer selection, collaboration, and campaign evaluation. This exercise will prepare you to leverage influencer marketing effectively in real-world scenarios.

2.7 Affiliate Marketing

Affiliate Marketing is a performance-based marketing strategy where businesses reward affiliates (partners or individuals) for driving traffic or sales to their website through the affiliate's marketing efforts. It's a win-win model, as affiliates earn commissions for their promotional efforts, while businesses benefit from increased sales.

Key Elements of Affiliate Marketing:

Affiliate Recruitment: Businesses recruit affiliates who have an audience or platform suitable for their products or services.

Affiliate Links: Affiliates use unique tracking links provided by businesses to promote products or services.

Commissions: Affiliates earn commissions for each sale or action generated through their affiliate links.

Payment Structure: Payment structures vary and can include pay-per-sale, pay-per-click, or pay-per-lead.

Tracking and Analytics: Accurate tracking and reporting are crucial to monitor affiliate performance.

Why Affiliate Marketing Matters:

Cost-Effective: Businesses only pay affiliates when they drive a desired action, making it a cost-effective marketing method.

Expanded Reach: Affiliates can extend a brand's reach to new audiences.

Performance-Based: Affiliate marketing is results-oriented, with clear metrics to measure success.

Diverse Promotion: Affiliates use various promotional methods, including blogs, social media, email, and websites.

Real-Life Success Story:

Case Study: Amazon Associates Program

Amazon's Affiliate Program, known as Amazon Associates, is one of the most well-known affiliate marketing success stories. Affiliates promote Amazon products on their websites, earning commissions for each sale generated through their affiliate links. Many affiliates have built lucrative businesses around this program.

Real-Life Task: Plan an Affiliate Marketing Campaign

To gain practical experience in affiliate marketing, create a mock affiliate marketing campaign for a fictional product or brand. Follow these steps:

Task: Plan an Affiliate Marketing Campaign

-

Choose a Product/Brand: Select a fictional product or brand to promote through affiliate marketing.

-
-

Identify Target Audience: Define the target audience for your product or brand. This will guide your affiliate recruitment.

-
-

Affiliate Recruitment: Identify fictional affiliates who have platforms or audiences aligned with your target demographic.

-
-

Campaign Objectives: Determine the objectives of your campaign. Are you aiming for increased sales, lead generation, or website traffic?

-
-

Affiliate Onboarding: Develop an onboarding process for your fictional affiliates, providing them with affiliate links and marketing materials.

-
-

Tracking and Reporting: Set up tracking systems to monitor affiliate performance and commissions.

-
-

Payment Structure: Define the payment structure for your fictional affiliates. Will it be pay-per-sale, pay-per-lead, or another model?

.

.

Analysis and Reflection: After the campaign, analyze the results and reflect on what worked well and what could be improved.

.

Creating a mock affiliate marketing campaign will equip you with practical skills in affiliate recruitment, tracking, and campaign optimization. This exercise will prepare you to effectively implement affiliate marketing strategies in real-world scenarios.

In the upcoming chapters, we will explore additional digital marketing services and strategies employed by digital marketing agencies, providing you with a comprehensive understanding of the digital marketing landscape.

Our journey through the world of digital marketing continues with a focus on two powerful strategies: Video Marketing and Mobile Marketing.

2.8 Video Marketing

Video Marketing is the use of videos to promote products, services, or brands to a target audience. It has become a dominant form of content marketing due to its ability to engage, educate, and entertain. Let's explore the key elements, significance, and real-life success stories of Video Marketing.

Key Elements of Video Marketing:

Content Creation: Creating compelling video content that resonates with the target audience is crucial. This includes video ads, product demos, tutorials, vlogs, and more.

Distribution Channels: Videos can be shared on various platforms, such as YouTube, social media, websites, and email marketing campaigns.

Storytelling: Effective video marketing often involves storytelling to connect with viewers on an emotional level.

Call to Action (CTA): Encourage viewers to take specific actions, such as subscribing, sharing, or making a purchase, through well-placed CTAs.

Why Video Marketing Matters:

High Engagement: Videos capture attention and keep viewers engaged for longer periods than text or images.

Versatility: Video content can be used for different marketing goals, including brand awareness, product promotion, and educational content.

SEO Benefits: Video can improve a website's search engine ranking and visibility.

Mobile Accessibility: With the rise of mobile devices, video content is easily accessible to a broad audience.

Real-Life Success Story:

Case Study: GoPro

GoPro, a company specializing in action cameras, has leveraged video marketing exceptionally well. They encourage users to share their GoPro-captured experiences, resulting in a vast library of user-generated content that showcases the product's capabilities. This strategy not only promotes the product but also builds a strong community around the brand.

Real-Life Task: Create a Video Marketing Campaign

To gain practical experience in video marketing, create a mock video marketing campaign for a fictional product or brand. Follow these steps:

Task: Create a Video Marketing Campaign

-

Choose a Product/Brand: Select a fictional product or brand to promote through video marketing.

-
-

Define Campaign Goals: Determine the objectives of your video marketing campaign. Are you aiming for brand awareness, product promotion, or engagement?

-
-

Audience Research: Understand your target audience's preferences, pain points, and interests to create content that resonates.

-
-

Content Creation: Produce a video that aligns with your campaign goals and audience insights. It can be a promotional video, how-to tutorial, or a compelling story.

Distribution Strategy: Decide where you'll share your video – on YouTube, social media, or your website. Consider any paid promotion if it's fictional.

CTA Implementation: Include a clear CTA within the video or its description to guide viewers on the desired action.

Analytics and Evaluation: Use analytics tools to track the video's performance, including views, engagement, and conversions.

Analysis and Reflection: After the campaign, analyze the results and reflect on what worked well and what could be improved.

Creating a mock video marketing campaign will equip you with practical skills in video creation, distribution, and campaign analysis. This exercise will prepare you to implement video marketing strategies effectively in real-world scenarios.

2.9 Mobile Marketing

Mobile Marketing is a strategy focused on reaching and engaging audiences on mobile devices, such as smartphones and tablets. Given the prevalence of mobile usage, understanding the key elements and significance of mobile marketing is crucial.

Key Elements of Mobile Marketing:

.

Mobile-Friendly Content: Ensure that websites, emails, and advertisements are mobile-responsive and provide an optimal user experience on smaller screens.

.

.

SMS Marketing: Send targeted text messages to subscribers for promotions, reminders, or updates.

.

.

In-App Advertising: Reach users through ads within mobile apps, leveraging the app's audience.

.

.

Location-Based Marketing: Use location data to deliver relevant content or offers to users based on their geographic location.

.

Why Mobile Marketing Matters:

.

Mobile Dominance: Mobile devices are the primary means of online access for many users worldwide.

Instant Connectivity: Mobile marketing allows brands to connect with users in real-time, increasing the chances of immediate engagement.

Personalization: Leveraging mobile data allows for

personalized and location-specific marketing.

App Utilization: Mobile apps provide a dedicated platform for reaching engaged users.

.

Real-Life Success Story:

Case Study: Starbucks

Starbucks, the global coffeehouse chain, has excelled in mobile marketing through its mobile app. The app offers features like mobile ordering, payment, and personalized recommendations. This strategy has not only improved customer convenience but also increased loyalty and sales.

Real-Life Task: Develop a Mobile Marketing Strategy

To gain practical experience in mobile marketing, create a mock mobile marketing strategy for a fictional product or brand. Follow these steps:

Task: Develop a Mobile Marketing Strategy

.

Choose a Product/Brand: Select a fictional product or brand to promote through mobile marketing.

.

.

Define Campaign Goals: Determine the objectives of your mobile marketing strategy. Are you aiming to drive app downloads, increase mobile sales, or improve customer engagement?

.

.

Audience Segmentation: Segment your fictional audience

based on demographics, behaviors, or location for targeted mobile marketing.

-
-

Content Creation: Create mobile-responsive content, which could include mobile ads, SMS messages, or in-app promotions.

-
-

Channel Selection: Choose the mobile channels you'll utilize, such as mobile apps, SMS, or location-based marketing.

-
-

CTA and Engagement: Implement clear CTAs to guide users on desired actions within the mobile experience.

-
-

Analytics and Optimization: Use mobile analytics to track the success of your strategy. Optimize based on user engagement and conversion data.

-
-

Analysis and Reflection: After the campaign, analyze the results and reflect on what worked well and what could be improved.

-

Developing a mock mobile marketing strategy will equip you with practical skills in mobile content creation, audience segmentation, and campaign evaluation. This exercise will prepare you to effectively leverage mobile marketing in real-world scenarios.

In the subsequent chapters, we will explore additional digital marketing services and strategies employed by digital marketing agencies, providing you with a comprehensive understanding of the digital marketing landscape.

Our exploration of digital marketing services continues with a focus on Analytics and Data-driven Marketing. In today's data-rich environment, harnessing the power of data is essential for effective decision-making and campaign optimization.

2.10 Analytics and Data-driven Marketing

Analytics and Data-driven Marketing involve the collection, analysis, and interpretation of data to make informed marketing decisions. This data-centric approach allows businesses to refine their strategies, target audiences more effectively, and achieve better campaign outcomes.

Key Elements of Analytics and Data-driven Marketing:

- **Data Collection:** Gather data from various sources, including website analytics, social media metrics, email campaign results, and customer behavior.

- **Data Analysis:** Utilize tools and platforms to analyze data and extract valuable insights.

- **Segmentation:** Divide audiences into segments based on demographics, behavior, preferences, or other criteria.

Personalization: Tailor marketing campaigns and messages to specific audience segments for increased relevance.

.

Why Analytics and Data-driven Marketing Matter:

.

Informed Decision-making: Data-driven insights enable marketers to make informed choices, optimizing campaign performance.

Efficiency: Targeting the right audience with personalized messages improves efficiency and reduces wasted marketing spend.

Competitive Advantage: Businesses that embrace data-driven marketing gain a competitive edge by staying ahead of market trends.

Customer Understanding: Deeper insights into customer behavior and preferences lead to improved customer experiences.

.

Real-Life Success Story:

Case Study: Netflix

Netflix, the streaming giant, relies heavily on data-driven marketing to personalize content recommendations for its users. By analyzing user viewing habits and preferences, Netflix suggests movies and TV shows tailored to individual tastes. This approach has significantly contributed to their success and customer retention.

Real-Life Task: Implement Data-driven Marketing

To gain practical experience in data-driven marketing, create a mock data-driven marketing strategy for a fictional product or brand. Follow these steps:

Task: Implement Data-driven Marketing

.

Choose a Product/Brand: Select a fictional product or brand to promote through data-driven marketing.

.

.

Define Campaign Goals: Determine the objectives of your data-driven marketing strategy. Are you aiming to improve conversion rates, increase customer retention, or enhance personalization?

.

.

Data Sources: Identify fictional data sources relevant to your strategy. This could include website analytics, customer surveys, or social media data.

.

.

Data Analysis: Analyze the selected data sources to extract insights and patterns that can guide your marketing decisions.

.

.

Audience Segmentation: Segment your fictional audience based on the insights derived from your data analysis.

.

.

Personalization: Develop personalized marketing messages or recommendations tailored to each audience segment.

.

.

Campaign Execution: Implement your data-driven marketing strategy across relevant channels, such as email, website, or social media.

Monitoring and Optimization: Continuously monitor campaign performance and make adjustments based on real-time data.

Analysis and Reflection: After the campaign, analyze the results and reflect on what worked well and what could be improved.

Executing a mock data-driven marketing strategy will provide hands-on experience in data analysis, audience segmentation, and campaign optimization. This exercise will prepare you to harness the power of data-driven marketing in real-world marketing scenarios.

In the upcoming chapters, we will explore additional digital marketing services and strategies employed by digital marketing agencies, providing you with a comprehensive understanding of the digital marketing landscape.

Chapter Three

Starting a Digital Marketing Agency

In this chapter, we will embark on an entrepreneurial journey to explore the key aspects of starting a digital marketing agency. Successful agencies are built on solid business planning and strategy, so let's dive into the essential steps, strategies, and real-life success stories to guide you on this path.

3.1 Business Planning and Strategy

Before launching a digital marketing agency, meticulous planning and a clear strategy are paramount. This section will cover the foundational steps to establish your agency and set it on a path to success.

Key Elements of Business Planning and Strategy:

·

Business Vision and Mission: Define the agency's purpose, values, and long-term goals.

·

Market Research: Conduct thorough research on your target market, including competitors and industry trends.

·

Service Offerings: Determine the digital marketing services your agency will specialize in, such as SEO, social media management, content marketing, or PPC advertising.

·

Target Audience: Identify the ideal client personas your agency aims to serve.

·

Pricing Strategy: Establish competitive and sustainable pricing models for your services.

·

Legal Structure: Choose the legal structure for your agency, such as a sole proprietorship, LLC, or corporation.

·

Business Plan: Develop a comprehensive business plan that outlines your agency's goals, strategies, financial projections, and marketing approach.

·

Why Business Planning and Strategy Matter:

Direction: A well-defined business plan provides a clear roadmap for your agency's growth and development.

Competitive Edge: Thorough research and strategic planning give your agency a competitive advantage in the market.

Resource Allocation: It helps allocate resources efficiently and avoid wasted efforts.

Goal Achievement: Effective planning and strategy execution lead to achieving business goals and objectives.

Real-Life Success Story:

Case Study: HubSpot

HubSpot, a leading inbound marketing, sales, and customer service platform, started as a marketing agency called HubSpot Inbound Marketing. The agency's founders, Brian Halligan and Dharmesh Shah, identified a need for inbound marketing services. Through their own successful inbound marketing strategies, they attracted clients and built a thriving agency. Eventually, HubSpot transitioned into developing marketing software, which has become a major player in the industry.

Real-Life Task: Create a Business Plan

To gain practical experience in business planning, create a mock business plan for your fictional digital marketing agency. Follow these steps:

Task: Create a Business Plan for Your Digital Marketing Agency

Define Your Vision and Mission: Clearly articulate your agency's vision and mission statements.

·

·

Market Research: Conduct research on the digital marketing landscape in your chosen niche, including competitor analysis and industry trends.

·

·

Service Offerings: Determine the specific digital marketing services your agency will offer, considering your expertise and market demand.

·

·

Target Audience: Create detailed buyer personas for your ideal clients.

·

·

Pricing Strategy: Develop a pricing model that balances competitiveness with profitability.

·

·

Legal Structure: Choose a legal structure for your fictional agency and explain the rationale behind your choice.

·

·

Business Plan Document: Compile all the elements into a comprehensive business plan document, including financial projections for the first three years.

·

·

Presentation: Create a presentation summarizing the key points of your business plan.

·

·

Pitch: Present your business plan to a fictional panel of potential investors or stakeholders, highlighting the unique value proposition of your agency.

.

Developing a mock business plan will equip you with the skills needed to create a solid foundation for your digital marketing agency. This exercise will prepare you to navigate the complexities of real-world business planning and strategy implementation.

In the following chapters, we will continue to explore essential aspects of establishing and growing your digital marketing agency, including client acquisition, team building, and effective client management.

As we continue our journey into the world of launching a digital marketing agency, we delve into two crucial considerations: Legal and Regulatory Considerations and Choosing a Niche. These elements are essential for building a strong foundation for your agency's success.

3.2 Legal and Regulatory Considerations

Launching a digital marketing agency involves navigating a range of legal and regulatory requirements. Compliance with these considerations is vital to ensure the legitimacy and longevity of your agency. Let's explore the key aspects of this topic.

Key Elements of Legal and Regulatory Considerations:

.

Business Registration: Register your agency as a legal entity, such as a sole proprietorship, LLC, partnership, or corporation, based on your chosen structure.

-
-

Licenses and Permits: Determine if your agency requires specific licenses or permits to operate in your jurisdiction.

-
-

Contracts and Agreements: Draft comprehensive contracts and service agreements to protect both your agency and clients. These agreements should outline project scopes, fees, timelines, and expectations.

-
-

Data Protection and Privacy: Understand and comply with data protection laws, such as GDPR (General Data Protection Regulation) for European clients or HIPAA (Health Insurance Portability and Accountability Act) for healthcare-related projects.

-
-

Intellectual Property Rights: Safeguard your agency's intellectual property, including branding, content, and proprietary tools.

-
-

Taxation: Comply with tax regulations and consider consulting with an accountant or tax expert for guidance.

-
-

Insurance: Explore insurance options, such as professional liability insurance, to protect your agency from potential legal claims.

-

Why Legal and Regulatory Considerations Matter:

Legitimacy: Complying with legal requirements establishes your agency's legitimacy in the eyes of clients and partners.

Risk Mitigation: Proper contracts and agreements reduce the risk of disputes and legal challenges.

Client Trust: Data protection and privacy compliance build trust with clients who entrust you with their data.

Financial Stability: Understanding tax obligations and having the right insurance coverage contributes to your agency's financial stability.

Real-Life Success Story:

Case Study: Moz

Moz, a renowned digital marketing software company, provides SEO tools and resources. While Moz is primarily known for its software, it initially started as an SEO consulting firm. Co-founder Rand Fishkin emphasizes the importance of legal considerations. In the early days of the business, they encountered legal issues related to contracts and client agreements. These experiences led to the development of standardized, legally sound contracts, which ultimately contributed to Moz's growth and success.

Real-Life Task: Navigate Legal Requirements

To gain practical experience in managing legal and regulatory considerations, complete a mock legal compliance checklist for your fictional digital marketing agency. Follow these steps:

Task: Navigate Legal and Regulatory Considerations

- **Business Structure:** Select a fictional legal structure for your agency and outline the steps needed to register it in your chosen jurisdiction.

- **Licenses and Permits:** Identify any fictional licenses or permits your agency may need to operate and list the requirements for obtaining them.

- **Sample Contracts:** Create sample contracts or service agreements that your fictional agency will use in client engagements. Ensure they cover essential aspects like project scope, deliverables, timelines, and payment terms.

- **Data Protection Policy:** Draft a fictional data protection and privacy policy for your agency, outlining how you handle client data in compliance with relevant regulations.

- **Intellectual Property Protection:** Develop a strategy for safeguarding your fictional agency's intellectual property rights, including branding and content.

- **Tax and Insurance:** Research fictional tax obligations and insurance options for your agency, considering factors like location and business structure.

- **Documentation:** Compile all your findings and documents into a comprehensive mock legal compliance checklist.

This mock legal compliance checklist will provide you with valuable insights into the legal aspects of running a digital marketing agency. It will help you understand the importance of adhering to legal and regulatory requirements while maintaining a solid legal foundation for your agency.

3.3 Choosing a Niche

Choosing a niche is a pivotal decision that can significantly impact your agency's success. Specializing in a specific industry or market segment allows you to tailor your services and become an expert in your chosen niche.

Key Elements of Choosing a Niche:

Market Research: Conduct research to identify industries or sectors with specific digital marketing needs and opportunities.

Passion and Expertise: Consider your passion and expertise when selecting a niche, as your enthusiasm will drive your agency's success.

Client Demands: Analyze the demand for digital marketing services within your chosen niche and identify gaps or underserved areas.

Competition: Evaluate the level of competition within your chosen niche and assess your agency's ability to differentiate itself.

.

.

Long-Term Viability: Assess the long-term viability and growth potential of your chosen niche.

.

Why Choosing a Niche Matters:

.

Expertise: Focusing on a niche allows you to become an expert in that field, making it easier to attract clients seeking specialized services.

Effective Marketing: Tailored marketing strategies and content resonate more with niche-specific audiences.

Reduced Competition: Specializing in a niche often means facing less competition than in broader markets.

Client Trust: Clients in the niche are more likely to trust and choose agencies with expertise in their industry.

.

Real-Life Success Story:

Case Study: Neil Patel

Neil Patel, a prominent digital marketing influencer and entrepreneur, has successfully carved a niche for himself in the competitive digital marketing space. His niche focuses on content marketing, SEO, and digital marketing education. Neil Patel's expertise and dedication to producing valuable content have positioned him as a trusted authority in these areas.

Real-Life Task: Select a Niche

To gain practical experience in choosing a niche for your

fictional digital marketing agency, follow these steps:

Task: Select a Niche for Your Digital Marketing Agency

Niche Identification: Identify a fictional niche for your agency. Consider your interests, expertise, and market research findings.

Market Research: Conduct mock market research to validate your chosen niche, including demand analysis and competitor assessment.

Client Persona: Create a fictional client persona within your chosen niche. Describe their industry-specific needs and pain points.

Unique Value Proposition: Define your agency's unique value proposition within the chosen niche. What sets you apart from competitors?

Marketing Strategy: Develop a fictional marketing strategy tailored to your niche, including content ideas, keywords, and outreach plans.

Long-Term Vision: Describe your agency's long-term vision within the chosen niche and how you plan to establish yourself as a niche leader.

Selecting a niche and creating a strategy around it will provide you with a deeper understanding of how specialization can benefit your agency. This exercise will help you make informed decisions about the direction and positioning of your fictional digital marketing agency.

In the following chapters, we will continue to explore essential aspects of starting and running a successful digital marketing agency, including client acquisition strategies, team building, and client management best practices.

3.4 Building a Digital Marketing Team

We shift our focus to the heart of any successful digital marketing agency: the team. Building a skilled and cohesive team is essential for delivering high-quality services and driving client success. We'll explore how to assemble your dream team, along with the tools and software necessary for efficient operations.

Building a Team

Building a team for your digital marketing agency requires careful consideration of roles, skills, and team dynamics. Your team will be the driving force behind client success, so let's delve into the key aspects of team building.

Key Elements of Building a Team:

- **Roles and Responsibilities:** Define the roles you need in your team, such as SEO specialists, content writers, social media managers, and project managers.

Skills and Expertise: Identify the specific skills and expertise required for each role and assess potential team members accordingly.

.

.

Recruitment: Develop a recruitment strategy to attract top talent. This may involve job postings, networking, or working with recruitment agencies.

.

.

Onboarding and Training: Create an onboarding process and training programs to ensure new team members understand your agency's culture and processes.

.

.

Team Dynamics: Foster a collaborative and positive team culture where members support one another's growth and success.

.

Why Building a Team Matters:

.

Expertise: A diverse team brings a range of skills and perspectives, enhancing the quality of work delivered to clients.

Scalability: A well-structured team allows your agency to take on more clients and larger projects.

Client Satisfaction: A competent team ensures client expectations are met and exceeded, leading to long-term client relationships.

Innovation: Collaboration within the team can lead to innovative solutions and strategies.

.

Real-Life Success Story:

Case Study: Semrush

Semrush, a leading digital marketing software company, attributes a significant part of its success to its talented team. They have a diverse team of experts in various fields, including SEO, content marketing, and analytics. This team works collaboratively to develop and improve their digital marketing tools, making them an industry leader.

Real-Life Task: Build a Mock Digital Marketing Team

To gain practical experience in building a digital marketing team, create a mock team structure for your fictional digital marketing agency. Follow these steps:

Task: Build a Mock Digital Marketing Team

-

Roles and Responsibilities: Define the roles needed in your fictional agency team, including titles, responsibilities, and reporting structures.

-

-

Skills and Expertise: Identify the specific skills and expertise required for each role. Consider what qualities make an ideal team member for each position.

-

Recruitment Strategy: Develop a fictional recruitment strategy for each role, outlining the channels and methods you would use to find potential candidates.

-

.

Team Dynamics: Describe the team culture and dynamics you want to cultivate within your fictional agency. How will team members collaborate and support each other?

.

.

Onboarding and Training: Outline a fictional onboarding process and training programs for new team members. Consider how you would ensure they align with your agency's values and standards.

.

Building a mock digital marketing team will help you understand the intricacies of team structure and dynamics. It's a valuable exercise for planning the growth and success of your fictional agency.

3.5 Tools and Software

Efficiency and effectiveness in digital marketing heavily rely on the right tools and software. In this section, we'll explore the essential tools and software solutions that can streamline your agency's operations and boost productivity.

Key Elements of Tools and Software:

.

SEO Tools: Utilize SEO tools like Moz, Ahrefs, or SEMrush for keyword research, site audits, and backlink analysis.

.

.

Content Management Systems (CMS): Choose a CMS like WordPress, Drupal, or Joomla for content creation and website management.

.

Social Media Management Platforms: Use tools like Hootsuite or Buffer to schedule posts, monitor social media engagement, and analyze performance.

Email Marketing Software: Platforms like Mailchimp or HubSpot can help automate email campaigns and track their effectiveness.

Analytics Tools: Google Analytics and Google Search Console provide valuable insights into website traffic and performance.

Project Management Software: Tools like Trello, Asana, or Monday.com help manage projects, tasks, and team collaboration.

Why Tools and Software Matter:

Efficiency: The right tools automate tasks, saving time and reducing manual workloads.

Data Analysis: Analytics tools provide valuable data for informed decision-making.

Competitive Advantage: Agencies with access to the latest digital marketing tools can offer clients a competitive edge.

Client Reporting: Reporting tools simplify the process of creating and sharing performance reports with clients.

Real-Life Success Story:

Case Study: Buffer

Buffer, a social media management platform, helps digital marketing agencies and businesses streamline their social media efforts. Through features like scheduling and analytics, Buffer has become an essential tool for social media management. Many agencies attribute their success in managing multiple social media accounts to Buffer's efficiency.

Real-Life Task: Explore Digital Marketing Tools

To gain practical experience with digital marketing tools, explore some of the key tools mentioned in this section. You can often access free trials or limited versions of these tools to familiarize yourself with their features. Consider the following:

Task: Explore Digital Marketing Tools

.

Choose a Tool: Select one of the digital marketing tools or software mentioned in this section that aligns with your fictional agency's services.

.

.

Free Trial: If available, sign up for a free trial or demo of the tool to explore its features.

.

.

Mock Campaign: Create a mock digital marketing campaign for your fictional agency using the chosen tool. Experiment with its capabilities and assess how it could benefit your agency's operations.

.

.

Feedback: Write a brief evaluation of the tool, highlighting its strengths and potential areas for improvement. Consider how it might enhance your fictional agency's services.

.

Exploring digital marketing tools will equip you with valuable insights into how these tools can enhance your agency's efficiency and capabilities. It will also help you make informed decisions about the tools you may choose to incorporate into your fictional agency's workflow.

In the upcoming chapters, we will continue our journey into the world of digital marketing agencies, covering topics like client acquisition, client management, and scaling your agency for growth

3.6 Setting Pricing and Packages

Pricing your digital marketing services effectively and crafting enticing packages are pivotal for attracting and retaining clients. In this chapter, we explore strategies for setting the right prices and creating appealing service packages to meet the diverse needs of your clients.

Pricing your services requires a balance between competitiveness, profitability, and client value. Additionally, creating well-structured packages can simplify the decision-making process for potential clients. Let's delve into these key aspects.

Key Elements of Setting Pricing and Packages:

.

Pricing Strategies: Explore various pricing models, such as hourly rates, project-based pricing, or retainer models.

.

.

Cost Analysis: Calculate your agency's operational costs to ensure pricing covers expenses while allowing for profitability.

Value-Based Pricing: Consider pricing based on the value your services provide to clients rather than just cost-plus pricing.

Tiered Packages: Develop tiered service packages with different levels of features and pricing to cater to a wider range of clients.

Client Education: Communicate the value of your services clearly to potential clients to justify your pricing.

Why Setting Pricing and Packages Matters:

Profitability: Effective pricing ensures your agency remains financially sustainable and profitable.

Client Attraction: Well-structured packages make it easier for potential clients to choose your services.

Client Retention: Packages that deliver value can lead to long-term client relationships.

Competitive Advantage: Strategic pricing can set you apart from competitors.

Real-Life Success Story:

Case Study: Neil Patel's Pricing Strategy

Digital marketing influencer Neil Patel offers a range of services, including SEO, content marketing, and social media marketing. Patel's pricing strategy is value-based, focusing on the results he can deliver to clients rather than hourly rates. By clearly articulating the value of his services and demonstrating his expertise, Patel has attracted high-profile clients and built a successful agency.

Real-Life Task: Develop Service Packages

To gain practical experience in setting pricing and creating service packages, follow these steps:

Task: Develop Service Packages for Your Digital Marketing Agency

.

Service Offerings: List the digital marketing services your fictional agency provides, such as SEO, content marketing, social media management, and PPC advertising.

.

.

Pricing Models: Explore different pricing models for each service, considering factors like hourly rates, project-based pricing, or retainer models.

.

.

Tiered Packages: Create at least three tiered service packages for one of your core services. Include varying levels of features and pricing for each package.

.

.

Value Proposition: Craft compelling value propositions for each package, highlighting the benefits and outcomes clients can expect.

-
-

Pricing Justification: Develop a brief strategy for justifying your pricing to potential clients. How will you communicate the value of your services?

-

Creating service packages will allow you to offer clients options that align with their needs and budgets. It's a valuable exercise for pricing strategy development and client acquisition.

3.7 Sales and Marketing for Your Agency

Effective sales and marketing strategies are fundamental to attracting and retaining clients. In this section, we'll explore strategies to promote your agency's services and convert leads into loyal clients.

Key Elements of Sales and Marketing:

-

Client Acquisition Channels: Identify the most effective channels for acquiring clients, such as content marketing, social media, email marketing, or networking.

-
-

Lead Generation: Develop lead generation strategies to attract potential clients to your agency.

-
-

Sales Techniques: Master sales techniques to convert leads into clients effectively.

-
-

Client Relationship Management: Implement strategies for nurturing client relationships and fostering long-term loyalty.

.

.

Content Marketing: Utilize content marketing to demonstrate your agency's expertise and attract potential clients.

.

Why Sales and Marketing Matter:

.

Client Base: Effective sales and marketing expand your agency's client base.

Revenue Growth: Successful lead generation and conversion increase revenue.

Client Retention: Strong client relationships lead to repeat business and referrals.

Brand Reputation: Consistent marketing efforts build your agency's reputation and authority in the industry.

.

Real-Life Success Story:

Case Study: Moz's Content Marketing Strategy

Moz, a prominent digital marketing software company, attributes much of its success to its content marketing efforts. They provide valuable resources, including blog posts, guides, and webinars, to educate and engage their audience. This content not only showcases their expertise but also attracts potential clients who are looking for digital marketing solutions.

Real-Life Task: Develop a Marketing Plan

To gain practical experience in developing a marketing plan, follow these steps:

Task: Develop a Marketing Plan for Your Digital Marketing Agency

.

Client Acquisition Channels: Choose two primary client acquisition channels, such as content marketing and social media.

.

.

Lead Generation: Develop strategies for lead generation within your chosen channels. For example, if you select content marketing, outline a content calendar with topics and publication schedules.

.

.

Sales Techniques: Create a mock sales script or strategy for converting leads into clients. Consider key talking points and objection-handling techniques.

.

.

Client Relationship Management: Develop a strategy for maintaining and nurturing client relationships. This could include regular check-ins, reporting, or client-exclusive webinars.

.

.

Content Marketing: If applicable, outline a content marketing strategy. Decide on the types of content you'll produce, the platforms you'll use, and the frequency of publication.

.

.

Implementation Timeline: Create a timeline for implementing your marketing plan, including specific milestones and deadlines.

.

A well-thought-out marketing plan is essential for attracting and retaining clients. This task will help you gain practical experience in developing a comprehensive marketing strategy for your fictional agency.

In the upcoming chapters, we'll explore client management, scaling your agency, and staying ahead in the ever-evolving landscape of digital marketing.

Chapter Four

Client Acquisition and Retention

In this chapter, we delve into the critical aspects of acquiring and retaining clients for your digital marketing agency. The ability to identify and attract the right clients is essential for the growth and sustainability of your agency.

4.1 Identifying Target Clients

Before you can successfully acquire and retain clients, you must first identify your ideal target clients. This process involves understanding your agency's strengths, the industries you excel in, and the specific client profiles that align with your expertise.

Key Elements of Identifying Target Clients:

- **Agency Strengths:** Define your agency's core strengths, whether it's SEO, content marketing, social media, or other services.

- **Industry Focus:** Determine the industries or niches in which your agency has expertise and can deliver exceptional results.

- **Client Profiles:** Create detailed client personas based on your strengths and industry focus. Consider factors such as company size, industry, goals, pain points, and budget.

- **Competitive Analysis:** Research your competitors and identify gaps in their client offerings. These gaps may represent opportunities to target specific clients.

Why Identifying Target Clients Matters:

- **Efficient Marketing:** Focusing on target clients allows you to tailor your marketing efforts more effectively.

Higher Conversion Rates: Targeting clients who align with your strengths increases the likelihood of converting leads into clients.

Client Satisfaction: Clients that fit your agency's expertise are more likely to be satisfied with your services.

Long-Term Relationships: Identifying the right clients can lead to long-term, mutually beneficial relationships.

.

Real-Life Success Story:

Case Study: HubSpot's Targeted Marketing

HubSpot, a leading inbound marketing and sales software platform, excels at identifying and targeting clients who are a natural fit for their services. They have developed detailed buyer personas and create content and marketing campaigns that resonate with these personas. This targeted approach has contributed significantly to HubSpot's growth and success.

Real-Life Task: Create Client Personas

To gain practical experience in identifying target clients, follow these steps:

Task: Create Client Personas for Your Digital Marketing Agency

.

Agency Strengths: List the core strengths and services offered by your fictional agency, such as SEO, content marketing, or social media management.

.

.

Industry Focus: Determine one or two industries or niches where your agency excels.

.

.

Client Profiles: Create detailed client personas based on your strengths and industry focus. Include information such as company size, industry, goals, pain points, and estimated budget.

.

.

Competitive Analysis: Conduct a fictional competitive analysis to identify gaps in your competitors' client offerings. Note any opportunities to target specific clients that your competitors may have overlooked.

.

.

Value Proposition: Craft value propositions for each client persona, highlighting how your agency's expertise aligns with their needs and goals.

.

Creating client personas will help you visualize and understand the types of clients your agency should target. This exercise is a fundamental step in developing a client acquisition strategy that focuses your efforts on attracting the right clients.

In the subsequent chapters, we will explore client acquisition strategies, client relationship management, and the keys to long-term client retention.

4.2 Sales and Pitching Strategies

We dive into the art of sales and pitching strategies for your digital marketing agency. Effective sales techniques and persuasive pitches are crucial for turning potential clients into paying customers.

The success of your digital marketing agency heavily depends on your ability to sell your services effectively. Whether it's in-person meetings, phone calls, or written proposals, mastering the art of sales and pitching is a vital skill.

Key Elements of Sales and Pitching Strategies:

.

Understanding Client Needs: Before pitching your services, thoroughly understand the potential client's needs, pain points, and objectives.

.

.

Crafting Compelling Proposals: Create well-structured proposals that clearly communicate your agency's value, services, and pricing.

.

.

Effective Communication: Develop strong communication skills, including active listening, to build rapport and trust with potential clients.

.

.

Overcoming Objections: Prepare for common objections and develop strategies to address them convincingly.

.

.

Value Proposition: Highlight the unique value your agency brings to the table, showcasing how your services can achieve the client's goals.

.

Why Sales and Pitching Strategies Matter:

.

Client Conversion: Effective sales strategies lead to higher conversion rates, increasing your client base.

Client Satisfaction: Understanding client needs and delivering tailored proposals result in more satisfied clients.

Revenue Growth: Successful pitching leads to more business and revenue for your agency.

Competitive Advantage: Mastering sales and pitching sets you apart from competitors.

.

Real-Life Success Story:

Case Study: Brian Tracy's Sales Training

Brian Tracy, a renowned sales trainer and author, has helped countless businesses and individuals improve their sales techniques. His training programs emphasize understanding client needs, effective communication, and objection handling. Many businesses credit Brian Tracy's methods with significant increases in their sales and revenue.

Real-Life Task: Create a Mock Pitch

To gain practical experience in sales and pitching, follow these steps:

Task: Create a Mock Pitch for Your Digital Marketing Agency

.

Choose a Client Persona: Select one of the client personas you created in the previous chapter as the target for your mock pitch.

.

.

Research Client Needs: Research and identify specific pain points and objectives of your chosen client persona.

.

.

Craft a Pitch: Develop a persuasive pitch that addresses the client's needs and highlights your agency's value proposition. You can create a written proposal or script for an in-person or virtual pitch.

.

.

Objection Handling: Anticipate potential objections from the client and prepare responses to address them convincingly.

.

.

Delivery: If possible, practice delivering your pitch to a colleague or mentor for feedback. Focus on clear communication and building rapport.

.

Creating a mock pitch will help you refine your sales and pitching skills, allowing you to confidently approach potential clients in the future.

4.3 Client Onboarding

Client onboarding is a critical step in the client-agency relationship. A well-executed onboarding process sets the stage for a successful partnership and ensures clients have a positive experience from the start.

Key Elements of Client Onboarding:

.

Welcome Packet: Prepare a welcome packet that introduces your agency, team members, and the services you'll provide.

.

.

Client Education: Educate clients about the digital marketing strategies you'll implement, setting realistic expectations and goals.

.

.

Setting Objectives: Collaboratively define clear objectives and key performance indicators (KPIs) to measure success.

.

.

Communication Channels: Establish communication channels and protocols for regular updates and reporting.

.

.

Reporting and Metrics: Explain how you'll provide regular reports and insights into the performance of their digital marketing campaigns.

.

Why Client Onboarding Matters:

.

Client Retention: A positive onboarding experience fosters client satisfaction and increases the likelihood of long-term retention.

Clear Expectations: Setting clear expectations from the beginning helps avoid misunderstandings and disappointments.

Efficient Collaboration: A structured onboarding process streamlines collaboration between your agency and the client.

Transparency: Demonstrating transparency in your onboarding process builds trust with clients.

Real-Life Success Story:

Case Study: HubSpot's Onboarding Process

HubSpot, a leading inbound marketing and sales software platform, is known for its client-centric onboarding process. They assign a dedicated onboarding specialist to each new client, guiding them through the setup process, training, and campaign launch. This hands-on approach has contributed to their high client satisfaction and retention rates.

Real-Life Task: Develop a Client Onboarding Checklist

To gain practical experience in client onboarding, follow these steps:

Task: Develop a Client Onboarding Checklist for Your Digital Marketing Agency

Welcome Packet: Create a welcome packet template that you would provide to new clients. Include an introduction to your agency, key team members, and an overview of services.

Client Education: Outline a document or presentation that educates clients about the digital marketing strategies you'll implement. Include examples and case studies.

Setting Objectives: Develop a template for setting objectives and KPIs with clients. Include a process for collaborative goal-setting.

·

·

Communication Channels: Define communication channels and protocols for client updates and reporting. Create templates for regular progress reports.

·

·

Client Feedback: Establish a system for collecting client feedback during the onboarding process to continuously improve your client onboarding experience.

·

Creating a client onboarding checklist will help ensure that every new client experiences a smooth and positive transition into your agency's services.

In the upcoming chapters, we will explore client management, scaling your agency, and strategies for long-term client retention.

4.4 Effective Communication

We delve into the art of effective communication, a cornerstone of building and maintaining long-term client relationships. Clear and transparent communication is essential for client satisfaction and trust.

Effective communication is the lifeblood of your client relationships. It involves not only conveying information but also active listening and understanding your clients' needs and concerns.

Key Elements of Effective Communication:

·

Active Listening: Develop active listening skills to fully understand your clients' perspectives and concerns.

.

.

Transparency: Be transparent about your strategies, progress, and any challenges your agency faces.

.

.

Regular Updates: Establish a schedule for providing regular updates and reporting on the status of clients' campaigns.

.

.

Client Feedback: Create mechanisms for clients to provide feedback, and be responsive to their suggestions and concerns.

.

.

Conflict Resolution: Develop strategies for resolving conflicts and addressing issues promptly and professionally.

.

Why Effective Communication Matters:

.

Client Trust: Transparent and open communication builds trust with clients.

Client Satisfaction: Satisfied clients are more likely to continue their partnership with your agency.

Problem Resolution: Effective communication allows you to address and resolve issues quickly.

Referrals: Happy clients are more likely to refer your agency to others.

.

Real-Life Success Story:

Case Study: Zappos' Customer Service

Zappos, an online shoe and clothing retailer, is known for its exceptional customer service and communication. They prioritize active listening to understand customer needs, and their representatives are encouraged to spend as much time as needed on phone calls, ensuring clients feel heard and valued. This commitment to communication has contributed to Zappos' loyal customer base.

Real-Life Task: Enhance Communication Skills

To gain practical experience in enhancing your communication skills, follow these steps:

Task: Conduct a Mock Client Meeting

.

Client Persona: Choose one of the client personas you created earlier for your mock client meeting.

.

.

Preparation: Prepare for the meeting as if it were a real client consultation. Research the industry, client's pain points, and goals.

.

.

Meeting Agenda: Create an agenda for the mock client meeting. Include a brief introduction, discussion of client goals, proposed strategies, and a question-and-answer session.

.

.

Active Listening: During the meeting, practice active listening by allowing the "client" to speak without interruption and asking clarifying questions.

-

-

Transparency: Be transparent about your agency's approach, strategies, and expected outcomes.

-

-

Conflict Resolution: Introduce a hypothetical challenge or concern and demonstrate how you would address it professionally and constructively.

-

-

Feedback: After the mock meeting, seek feedback from a colleague or mentor on your communication skills and the effectiveness of your communication during the meeting.

-

This exercise will help you refine your communication skills and prepare you for real client interactions.

4.5 Building Long-Term Client Relationships

Building long-term client relationships is the cornerstone of a successful digital marketing agency. These relationships can lead to repeat business, referrals, and a strong reputation in the industry.

Key Elements of Building Long-Term Client Relationships:

-

Consistency: Consistently deliver high-quality service and results to maintain trust.

-

-

Client-Centric Approach: Always prioritize the client's needs and goals.

-
-

Client Education: Educate clients about digital marketing strategies, progress, and industry trends.

-
-

Regular Check-Ins: Schedule regular check-ins to review performance, address concerns, and explore opportunities for improvement.

-
-

Going the Extra Mile: Occasionally go above and beyond to exceed client expectations.

-

Why Building Long-Term Client Relationships Matters:

-

Repeat Business: Satisfied clients are more likely to continue working with your agency on new projects.

Referrals: Long-term clients are more likely to refer your agency to other businesses.

Stability: A strong client base provides stability and a steady stream of revenue.

Positive Reputation: Long-term client relationships contribute to a positive agency reputation.

-

Real-Life Success Story:

Case Study: Ogilvy & Mather's Client Relationships

Ogilvy & Mather, a global advertising and marketing agency, is known for its enduring client relationships. Some of their clients have been with the agency for decades. This longevity is a testament to Ogilvy & Mather's commitment to delivering value and maintaining trust.

Real-Life Task: Develop a Client Retention Plan

To gain practical experience in building long-term client relationships, follow these steps:

Task: Develop a Client Retention Plan for Your Digital Marketing Agency

Client Selection: Choose one of your fictional clients from previous exercises.

Client Relationship Enhancement: Identify strategies to enhance your relationship with this client over the long term. Consider regular check-ins, educational resources, and added-value services.

Feedback Mechanism: Create a feedback mechanism to gather input from the client about their experience with your agency.

Value-Added Services: Brainstorm value-added services or offerings that you could provide to this client to exceed their expectations.

Referral Program: Consider implementing a referral program to encourage satisfied clients to refer others to your agency.

A well-thought-out client retention plan is essential for nurturing long-term relationships that benefit both your agency and your clients.

In the subsequent chapters, we'll explore scaling your agency, managing a team, and ensuring long-term success in the dynamic field of digital marketing.

4.6 Client Retention Strategies

We'll delve into client retention strategies—how to keep your existing clients satisfied and engaged. Client retention is a vital aspect of ensuring the long-term success and growth of your digital marketing agency.

Client retention involves nurturing your existing client relationships to ensure they continue working with your agency and ideally become advocates for your services.

Key Elements of Client Retention Strategies:

Regular Communication: Maintain open and consistent communication with your clients to stay informed about their evolving needs and challenges.

Value-Added Services: Offer additional services or resources that provide extra value and benefit to your clients.

Proactive Problem Solving: Anticipate potential issues and address them proactively to prevent client dissatisfaction.

Client Feedback: Continuously gather and act on client feedback to make improvements.

Personalization: Customize your approach and services to align with each client's unique goals and preferences.

Why Client Retention Strategies Matter:

Stability: Retained clients contribute to the stability and consistent revenue of your agency.

Referrals: Satisfied, long-term clients are more likely to refer your agency to others.

Cost Efficiency: Retaining clients is often more cost-effective than acquiring new ones.

Positive Reputation: Long-term client relationships contribute to a positive agency reputation.

Real-Life Success Story:

Case Study: Amazon Prime

Amazon Prime is a subscription service known for its exceptional client retention strategies. By offering a wide range of benefits, such as fast shipping, streaming content, and exclusive deals, Amazon Prime keeps subscribers engaged and loyal. The high retention rate of Prime members has been a significant factor in Amazon's success.

Real-Life Task: Develop a Client Retention Plan

To gain practical experience in client retention strategies, follow these steps:

Task: Develop a Client Retention Plan for Your Digital Marketing Agency

·

Client Selection: Choose one of your fictional clients from previous exercises.

·

·

Client Engagement: Identify strategies to keep this client engaged and satisfied over the long term. Consider additional services, educational resources, or personalized offerings.

·

·

Feedback Mechanism: Create a system for gathering regular feedback from the client about their experience with your agency. Consider using surveys or direct interviews.

·

·

Anticipate Challenges: Identify potential challenges that might arise during your client's partnership with your agency. Develop proactive solutions to address these issues.

·

·

Value-Added Services: Brainstorm value-added services or offerings that you could provide to this client to exceed their expectations and improve their experience.

·

A well-structured client retention plan is essential for nurturing and maintaining valuable long-term client relationships.

Leveraging Client Testimonials and Case Studies

Client testimonials and case studies are powerful tools for showcasing your agency's successes and building trust with potential clients. They provide real-world proof of your agency's capabilities and results.

Key Elements of Leveraging Client Testimonials and Case Studies:

- **Client Consent:** Obtain client consent to use their feedback and results in testimonials and case studies.

- **Success Stories:** Create detailed case studies that highlight the challenges your agency addressed and the positive outcomes achieved.

- **Variety of Mediums:** Present client testimonials and case studies in various formats, such as written testimonials, video interviews, and downloadable PDFs.

- **Placement:** Feature client testimonials and case studies prominently on your agency's website and marketing materials.

Why Leveraging Client Testimonials and Case Studies Matters:

-

Credibility: Client success stories lend credibility to your agency's claims and capabilities.

Proof of Results: Testimonials and case studies provide concrete evidence of your agency's ability to deliver results.

Influence Purchase Decisions: Prospective clients are more likely to trust and choose an agency with a track record of success.

Differentiation: Stand out from competitors by showcasing your unique successes and client stories.

-

Real-Life Success Story:

Case Study: Neil Patel's Content Marketing Success

Digital marketing expert Neil Patel often shares case studies and client testimonials to showcase the effectiveness of his agency's strategies. By highlighting specific results, such as significant traffic and revenue increases, he reinforces trust in his agency's expertise.

Real-Life Task: Create a Client Testimonial

To gain practical experience in leveraging client testimonials and case studies, follow these steps:

Task: Create a Mock Client Testimonial

-

Client Persona: Select one of your fictional clients as the subject of your mock client testimonial.

-

Client Consent: In a fictional scenario, obtain consent from your fictional client to use their feedback for a testimonial.

-
-

Success Story: Write a detailed testimonial that highlights the challenges the client faced, the strategies your agency implemented, and the positive results achieved.

-
-

Medium: Choose a format for your testimonial, such as a written testimonial, a video interview script, or a downloadable PDF.

-
-

Placement: Consider where you would feature this testimonial on your agency's website or marketing materials.

-

Creating a mock client testimonial will help you understand the process of gathering and presenting client feedback effectively.

In the following chapters, we will explore strategies for scaling your agency, managing a team, and ensuring long-term success in the dynamic field of digital marketing.

Chapter Five

Managing Digital Marketing Campaigns

In this chapter, we'll delve into the intricacies of managing digital marketing campaigns successfully. Effective campaign planning and strategy are essential to achieving your clients' goals and delivering results.

5.1 Campaign Planning and Strategy

Campaign planning and strategy are the foundation of any successful digital marketing endeavor. These processes guide the execution of campaigns and ensure alignment with client objectives.

Key Elements of Campaign Planning and Strategy:

- **Client Goals:** Clearly define the client's objectives and key performance indicators (KPIs) for the campaign.

- **Target Audience:** Identify the specific audience segments you intend to reach with the campaign.

- **Channel Selection:** Determine the digital channels (e.g., social media, email, search) that are most appropriate for reaching the target audience.

.

.

Content Strategy: Develop a content plan that outlines the type of content, messaging, and creative assets needed for the campaign.

.

.

Budget Allocation: Allocate the campaign budget effectively, considering the distribution of funds across channels and activities.

.

Why Campaign Planning and Strategy Matter:

.

Goal Alignment: Proper planning ensures that campaign activities align with the client's goals and objectives.

Efficiency: A well-structured plan streamlines the execution process and minimizes wasted resources.

Measurable Results: Clear objectives and KPIs enable you to measure the success of the campaign accurately.

Client Satisfaction: Successful campaigns that meet or exceed goals contribute to client satisfaction and retention.

.

Real-Life Success Story:

Case Study: Airbnb's "Live There" Campaign

Airbnb's "Live There" campaign is an example of effective campaign planning and strategy. The campaign aimed to shift the focus from touristy travel to experiencing destinations like a local. Airbnb carefully planned the campaign's messaging, content, and target audience to convey its unique value proposition. The result was a highly successful campaign that resonated with travelers and contributed to Airbnb's growth.

Real-Life Task: Develop a Campaign Strategy

To gain practical experience in campaign planning and strategy, follow these steps:

Task: Develop a Campaign Strategy for a Fictional Client

-
Client Persona: Choose one of your fictional clients or create a new one for this task.

-
-
Client Goals: Define specific goals and objectives that your fictional client wants to achieve through a digital marketing campaign. For example, increasing website traffic, generating leads, or boosting e-commerce sales.

-
-
Target Audience: Identify the target audience for the campaign. Consider demographics, interests, and online behaviors.

-
-
Channel Selection: Determine which digital channels (e.g., social media, email marketing, PPC advertising) are most suitable for reaching the target audience and achieving the client's goals.

-
-
Content Plan: Outline the content strategy for the campaign,

including messaging, creative assets, and the content calendar.

Budget Allocation: Allocate a hypothetical budget to different aspects of the campaign, such as advertising spend, content creation, and analytics tools.

KPIs: Define key performance indicators (KPIs) that will be used to measure the campaign's success.

Developing a campaign strategy for a fictional client will provide you with hands-on experience in creating comprehensive plans that align with client goals and objectives.

In the upcoming sections, we'll explore campaign execution, monitoring and optimization, and client reporting to ensure your digital marketing campaigns deliver exceptional results.

In this section, we'll continue our exploration of managing digital marketing campaigns by diving into two crucial components: keyword research and analysis, and content creation and optimization. These elements are essential for driving targeted traffic and achieving campaign goals.

Keyword Research and Analysis

Keyword research is the process of identifying the search terms and phrases that potential customers use when looking for products, services, or information online. Effective keyword research is the foundation of successful search engine optimization (SEO) and pay-per-click (PPC) campaigns.

Key Elements of Keyword Research and Analysis:

.

Understanding User Intent: Determine the intent behind user search queries (e.g., informational, transactional) to align keywords with user needs.

.

.

Keyword Tools: Utilize keyword research tools such as Google Keyword Planner, SEMrush, or Ahrefs to identify relevant keywords and assess their search volume and competition.

.

.

Competitor Analysis: Analyze competitor keywords to identify opportunities and gaps in your keyword strategy.

.

.

Long-Tail Keywords: Consider targeting long-tail keywords (more specific and less competitive) to capture niche audiences.

.

.

Keyword Mapping: Organize keywords into relevant groups to inform content creation and campaign structure.

.

Why Keyword Research and Analysis Matter:

.

Targeted Traffic: Well-researched keywords attract users genuinely interested in your offerings.

Improved Rankings: Proper keyword optimization can lead to higher search engine rankings.

Cost Efficiency: PPC campaigns benefit from targeting the most relevant keywords, reducing ad spend wastage.

Content Relevance: Keywords inform content creation,

ensuring that your content addresses user queries.

Real-Life Success Story:

Case Study: Moz's Keyword Explorer

Moz, a renowned SEO software company, developed the Keyword Explorer tool to simplify keyword research. The tool provides valuable data on keyword difficulty, search volume, and click-through rates. By using their own tool effectively, Moz demonstrates the power of keyword research in the SEO industry.

Real-Life Task: Conduct Keyword Research

To gain practical experience in keyword research, follow these steps:

Task: Conduct Keyword Research for a Fictional Client

Client Persona: Choose one of your fictional clients or create a new one for this task.

Industry Analysis: Research your client's industry to understand the main topics and trends relevant to their business.

Keyword Tools: Use a keyword research tool (e.g., Google Keyword Planner) to identify a list of potential keywords related to your client's products, services, or content.

.

Keyword Metrics: Assess the search volume, keyword difficulty, and competition level for each keyword.

.

Keyword Selection: Choose a set of primary and secondary keywords that align with your client's goals and target audience.

.

Keyword Mapping: Organize the selected keywords into categories or groups that will inform your content strategy and campaign structure.

.

Conducting keyword research for a fictional client will provide you with hands-on experience in identifying valuable keywords and laying the groundwork for effective digital marketing campaigns.

5.2 Content Creation and Optimization

Content is the heart of any digital marketing campaign. Creating high-quality, valuable content that resonates with your target audience is essential for driving engagement, building trust, and achieving campaign objectives.

Key Elements of Content Creation and Optimization:

.

Audience Persona: Develop detailed audience personas to tailor content to the specific needs and preferences of your target audience.

.

Content Formats: Consider various content formats, including blog posts, infographics, videos, and interactive content, to diversify your content strategy.

- **SEO Optimization:** Incorporate relevant keywords into your content naturally to improve search engine rankings.

- **Quality and Value:** Prioritize content quality and value to provide users with useful information or entertainment.

- **Consistency:** Maintain a regular content publishing schedule to keep your audience engaged.

Why Content Creation and Optimization Matter:

- **Audience Engagement:** High-quality content attracts and engages your target audience.

Brand Authority: Valuable content establishes your brand as an authority in your industry.

SEO Benefits: Well-optimized content improves search engine rankings and organic traffic.

Conversion: Compelling content can drive conversions and achieve campaign objectives.

Real-Life Success Story:

Case Study: HubSpot's Blog

HubSpot, a leading inbound marketing and sales platform,

has a highly successful blog that covers a wide range of topics related to marketing, sales, and customer service. Their content consistently provides value to their audience, positions HubSpot as an industry leader, and contributes to their lead generation efforts.

Real-Life Task: Create and Optimize Content

To gain practical experience in content creation and optimization, follow these steps:

Task: Create and Optimize a Blog Post for a Fictional Client

- **Client Persona:** Choose one of your fictional clients or create a new one for this task.

- **Topic Selection:** Select a topic that is relevant to your client's industry and aligns with their goals and audience.

- **Keyword Integration:** Incorporate the keywords you identified during the keyword research task naturally into the content.

- **Content Format:** Choose a content format (e.g., blog post) and create a piece of content that provides value to your target audience.

- **SEO Optimization:** Optimize the content for SEO by including relevant headers, meta descriptions, and alt text for images.

Publish and Promote: Publish the content on a fictional website or blog and promote it through social media or email marketing.

Creating and optimizing content for a fictional client will help you hone your content creation skills and understand the importance of aligning content with campaign goals and audience needs.

In the subsequent sections, we'll explore campaign execution, monitoring, and optimization to ensure that your digital marketing campaigns deliver exceptional results for your clients.

In this section, we'll continue our exploration of managing digital marketing campaigns by focusing on two critical aspects: social media management and paid advertising campaigns. These elements play a pivotal role in modern digital marketing strategies.

5.4 Social Media Management

Social media platforms are powerful channels for engaging with audiences, building brand awareness, and driving traffic. Effective social media management involves crafting compelling content, engaging with followers, and leveraging data to refine strategies.

Key Elements of Social Media Management:

Content Strategy: Develop a content plan that includes a mix of text, images, videos, and interactive content tailored to each platform.

.

.

Audience Engagement: Regularly respond to comments, messages, and interactions to foster community engagement.

.

.

Scheduling and Posting: Use social media management tools to schedule posts at optimal times for your audience.

.

.

Analytics and Insights: Analyze social media data to measure the performance of your content and campaigns.

.

.

Paid Social Advertising: Consider paid advertising on social platforms to reach a wider audience.

.

Why Social Media Management Matters:

.

Audience Reach: Social media platforms have billions of active users, providing a vast audience for your campaigns.

Brand Visibility: Consistent and engaging social media presence enhances brand visibility and recognition.

Community Building: Effective social media management fosters a sense of community among followers.

Conversion Opportunities: Social media can drive traffic and conversions when used strategically.

.

Real-Life Success Story:

Case Study: Wendy's Twitter Roasts

Wendy's, the fast-food chain, gained significant attention and engagement on Twitter through witty and humorous responses to customer tweets. This approach not only entertained followers but also boosted the brand's online presence and engagement.

Real-Life Task: Create a Social Media Content Plan

To gain practical experience in social media management, follow these steps:

Task: Develop a Social Media Content Plan for a Fictional Client

- **Client Persona:** Choose one of your fictional clients or create a new one for this task.

- **Platform Selection:** Identify the social media platforms most relevant to your client's target audience and goals.

- **Content Calendar:** Create a content calendar outlining the types of content you'll post on each platform, along with posting schedules.

- **Content Creation:** Develop or curate content that aligns with your client's brand and resonates with their audience.

- **Engagement Strategy:** Outline how you'll engage with followers, including responding to comments, messages, and interactions.

-
-

Analytics Plan: Define key performance indicators (KPIs) for measuring the success of your social media efforts.

-

Creating a social media content plan for a fictional client will help you understand the importance of consistency, audience engagement, and data analysis in social media management.

5.5 Paid Advertising Campaigns

Paid advertising campaigns, such as pay-per-click (PPC) advertising, offer businesses the opportunity to reach a targeted audience through platforms like Google Ads and social media advertising. Effective management of paid campaigns involves strategy, optimization, and monitoring.

Key Elements of Paid Advertising Campaigns:

-

Goal Setting: Clearly define campaign objectives, whether it's driving website traffic, generating leads, or boosting e-commerce sales.

-
-

Keyword Research: Select relevant keywords to target in PPC campaigns to ensure your ads reach the right audience.

-
-

Ad Creation: Craft compelling ad copy and visuals that resonate with your target audience and encourage clicks.

-

Budget Management: Allocate the campaign budget wisely, considering factors like bidding strategy and ad performance.

A/B Testing: Continuously test different ad variations to optimize performance and maximize return on investment (ROI).

Why Paid Advertising Campaigns Matter:

Targeted Reach: Paid advertising allows you to reach specific demographics and user groups.

Immediate Visibility: Ads can provide immediate visibility and results when managed effectively.

Data-Driven Decisions: Advertising platforms provide detailed data and insights for campaign optimization.

Scalability: Paid campaigns can be scaled up or down to align with campaign goals and budgets.

Real-Life Success Story:

Case Study: Dollar Shave Club's Video Ad

Dollar Shave Club's "Our Blades Are F***ing Great" video ad became a viral sensation. The company's humorous and memorable ad not only generated immense brand visibility but also drove significant sales, showcasing the power of effective paid advertising.

Real-Life Task: Create a Paid Advertising Campaign

To gain practical experience in managing paid advertising campaigns, follow these steps:

Task: Develop a Mock Paid Advertising Campaign for a Fictional Client

Client Persona: Choose one of your fictional clients or create a new one for this task.

Campaign Objective: Define a specific campaign objective, such as driving website visits, generating leads, or increasing online sales.

Platform Selection: Choose the most suitable advertising platform(s) for your campaign (e.g., Google Ads, Facebook Ads).

Keyword Research: Conduct keyword research to identify relevant keywords for your campaign.

Ad Creation: Develop ad copy and visuals that align with your campaign objective and target audience.

Budget Allocation: Determine the campaign budget and bidding strategy.

A/B Testing Plan: Create a plan for A/B testing different ad variations to optimize performance.

.

Executing a mock paid advertising campaign will provide you with hands-on experience in managing paid campaigns, including setting goals, creating ads, and monitoring performance.

In the following chapters, we'll explore campaign monitoring, optimization, and reporting to ensure your digital marketing campaigns continue to deliver exceptional results for your clients.

In this section, we'll continue our exploration of managing digital marketing campaigns by focusing on two vital components: email marketing campaigns and analytics and reporting. These elements are essential for measuring and optimizing campaign performance.

5.6 Email Marketing Campaigns

Email marketing remains a highly effective way to engage with your audience, nurture leads, and drive conversions. Successful email marketing campaigns involve crafting compelling emails, segmenting your audience, and analyzing performance metrics.

Key Elements of Email Marketing Campaigns:

.

Audience Segmentation: Divide your email list into segments based on factors such as demographics, behaviors, and interests.

.

.

Email Content: Create engaging email content, including subject lines, visuals, and compelling calls to action (CTAs).

.

.

Automation: Use email automation to send targeted messages at the right time, such as welcome emails or abandoned cart reminders.

A/B Testing: Continuously test different elements of your emails, such as subject lines, to optimize open and click-through rates.

Performance Metrics: Monitor key performance metrics like open rates, click-through rates, conversion rates, and unsubscribe rates.

Why Email Marketing Campaigns Matter:

Direct Communication: Email allows direct communication with your audience, fostering a sense of connection.

Lead Nurturing: Email is an effective tool for nurturing leads and guiding them through the customer journey.

Conversion Driver: Well-crafted emails can drive conversions, whether it's making a purchase or signing up for a webinar.

Personalization: Segmentation and personalization can improve email relevance and engagement.

Real-Life Success Story:

Case Study: Airbnb's Host Community Emails

Airbnb sends personalized emails to its host community, offering tips, support, and information tailored to each host's location and property type. These emails strengthen the host-host relationship and encourage engagement within the Airbnb platform.

Real-Life Task: Create an Email Marketing Campaign

To gain practical experience in email marketing, follow these steps:

Task: Develop an Email Marketing Campaign for a Fictional Client

.

Client Persona: Choose one of your fictional clients or create a new one for this task.

.

.

Campaign Objective: Define a specific campaign objective, such as promoting a product, driving traffic to a website, or nurturing leads.

.

.

Audience Segmentation: Segment your fictional client's email list into relevant categories or groups.

.

.

Email Content: Create an email with engaging content, including a subject line, visuals, and a clear call to action.

.

.

Automation: If applicable, set up automation triggers for the email campaign (e.g., welcome series, abandoned cart emails).

.

.

A/B Testing Plan: Plan A/B tests for elements like subject lines or CTA buttons to optimize email performance.

-
-

Performance Metrics: Define the key performance metrics you'll track to measure the success of your email campaign.

-

Creating an email marketing campaign for a fictional client will allow you to gain hands-on experience in crafting effective emails and understanding the importance of audience segmentation and performance analysis.

5.7 Analytics and Reporting

Effective campaign management relies on data-driven decisions. Analytics and reporting provide insights into campaign performance, helping you identify areas for improvement and optimization.

Key Elements of Analytics and Reporting:

-

Data Collection: Utilize analytics tools (e.g., Google Analytics, social media insights) to collect data on campaign performance.

-
-

Key Performance Indicators (KPIs): Define KPIs that align with your campaign objectives and goals.

-
-

Regular Reporting: Create regular reports that highlight campaign performance metrics, trends, and areas for improvement.

-

Data Interpretation: Analyze data to gain insights into audience behavior, conversion paths, and the effectiveness of various marketing channels.

Optimization Strategies: Use data insights to inform optimization strategies and refine campaign tactics.

Why Analytics and Reporting Matter:

Data-Driven Decisions: Analytics enable data-driven decisions for campaign optimization.

ROI Measurement: Reporting allows you to measure the return on investment (ROI) of your marketing efforts.

Continuous Improvement: Regular reporting helps identify what's working and what needs improvement.

Client Communication: Transparent reporting builds trust and transparency with clients.

Real-Life Success Story:

Case Study: Google Analytics

Google Analytics is a powerful tool used by businesses worldwide. It provides comprehensive data on website traffic, user behavior, and conversion tracking. Through data analysis and reporting, businesses can optimize their digital marketing efforts and achieve better results.

Real-Life Task: Create a Campaign Performance Report

To gain practical experience in analytics and reporting, follow these steps:

Task: Develop a Campaign Performance Report for a Fictional Client

.

Client Persona: Choose one of your fictional clients or create a new one for this task.

.

.

Campaign Selection: Select one of your fictional client's digital marketing campaigns to analyze.

.

.

KPI Definition: Define the key performance indicators (KPIs) that are most relevant to the chosen campaign.

.

.

Data Collection: Use relevant analytics tools to gather data on the campaign's performance.

.

.

Report Creation: Create a comprehensive report that includes an executive summary, KPI metrics, trends, and actionable insights.

.

.

Optimization Recommendations: Based on the data, provide recommendations for optimizing the campaign or future campaigns.

.

Developing a campaign performance report for a fictional client will give you hands-on experience in data analysis, reporting, and the ability to make informed decisions for campaign optimization.

In the upcoming chapters, we'll explore campaign monitoring and optimization strategies, ensuring that your digital marketing campaigns continue to evolve and deliver exceptional results for your clients.

[x]

Monitoring and Optimizing Digital Marketing Campaigns

In this section, we will delve into the crucial aspects of monitoring and optimizing digital marketing campaigns. This phase of campaign management is essential for ensuring that your efforts yield the best possible results for your clients.

5.8 Campaign Optimization and Performance Tracking

Campaign optimization involves making strategic adjustments to improve campaign performance. It requires a keen eye for data analysis and a proactive approach to tweaking various campaign elements.

Key Elements of Campaign Optimization:

.

Data Analysis: Regularly analyze campaign data to identify trends, strengths, and areas for improvement.

.

.

Conversion Rate Optimization (CRO): Focus on improving the conversion rate by enhancing landing pages, CTAs, and user experience.

.

.

Budget Reallocation: Adjust budget allocation based on the performance of different channels and campaigns.

.

.

A/B Testing: Continue A/B testing to refine ad copy, visuals, and landing page elements.

.

.

Keyword Optimization: Optimize keywords for better ad positioning and relevance.

.

Why Campaign Optimization Matters:

.

Improved ROI: Optimization efforts can lead to a higher return on investment (ROI).

Better User Experience: Optimized campaigns often result in a better user experience, leading to higher conversions.

Stay Competitive: In the ever-evolving digital landscape, staying competitive requires ongoing optimization.

.

Real-Life Success Story:

Case Study: Airbnb's A/B Testing

Airbnb frequently conducts A/B tests on its website and app to enhance user experience and conversion rates. Through rigorous testing of different elements, such as imagery and text, they continually improve their platform's performance.

Real-Life Task: Conduct a Campaign Optimization Analysis

To gain hands-on experience in campaign optimization, follow these steps:

Task: Analyze and Optimize a Fictional Client's Digital Marketing Campaign

.

Client Persona: Choose one of your fictional clients or create a new one for this task.

.

.

Campaign Selection: Select a digital marketing campaign for analysis and optimization.

.

.

Data Review: Review the campaign's data, including key performance indicators (KPIs), click-through rates, conversion rates, and budget allocation.

.

.

Identify Areas for Improvement: Based on the data, identify areas within the campaign that need improvement. This could include ad copy, landing pages, targeting, or budget allocation.

.

.

Develop an Optimization Plan: Create a detailed plan for optimizing the campaign. Specify the changes you will make, such as A/B testing ad variations, refining keyword targeting, or optimizing landing pages.

.

.

Implementation: Put your optimization plan into action, making the necessary adjustments to the campaign.

.

.

Monitor Results: After implementing changes, closely monitor the campaign's performance to assess the impact of your optimizations.

.

.

Report and Analysis: Create a report detailing the changes made, the results achieved, and recommendations for further optimization.

.

Conducting a campaign optimization analysis for a fictional client will provide you with valuable experience in data-driven decision-making and the practical application of optimization strategies.

In the following chapters, we will explore additional strategies for campaign management, including multi-channel marketing, remarketing, and the importance of client communication.

Chapter Six

Measuring Success and ROI

In this chapter, we'll dive into the critical process of measuring success and return on investment (ROI) in your digital marketing campaigns. Understanding how to gauge the effectiveness of your efforts is paramount to achieving and demonstrating value for your clients.

6.1 Key Performance Indicators (KPIs)

Key Performance Indicators (KPIs) are measurable metrics that reflect the performance and progress of your digital marketing campaigns. Selecting the right KPIs is crucial for evaluating the success of your campaigns and aligning your efforts with client goals.

Key Elements of Key Performance Indicators:

- **KPI Selection:** Choose KPIs that directly relate to your campaign objectives and client goals. Common KPIs include conversion rate, click-through rate (CTR), cost per acquisition (CPA), and return on ad spend (ROAS).

- **Data Tracking:** Implement robust tracking tools and analytics platforms to gather data accurately.

- **Benchmarking:** Establish benchmarks or baseline values for each KPI to measure progress and success.

- **Regular Monitoring:** Continuously monitor KPIs throughout the campaign duration to identify trends and areas for improvement.

- **Performance Analysis:** Analyze KPI data to draw insights into what's working and what needs adjustment.

-

Why Key Performance Indicators (KPIs) Matter:

Objective Assessment: KPIs provide an objective way to assess campaign performance.

Data-Driven Decisions: KPI data guides decision-making for campaign adjustments and optimization.

Client Alignment: Aligning campaign KPIs with client goals fosters transparency and trust.

Demonstrating ROI: KPIs are instrumental in showcasing the return on investment (ROI) of digital marketing efforts.

Real-Life Success Story:

Case Study: HubSpot's Conversion Rate Optimization

HubSpot, a marketing automation platform, used conversion rate optimization (CRO) to increase sign-up conversions for their free trial. By systematically testing and refining elements of their landing pages and CTAs, they achieved a 186% increase in sign-up conversions.

Real-Life Task: Define KPIs for a Campaign

To gain hands-on experience in defining KPIs, follow these steps:

Task: Define KPIs for a Fictional Client's Digital Marketing Campaign

Client Persona: Choose one of your fictional clients or create a new one for this task.

.

.

Campaign Objective: Determine the specific objective for the client's digital marketing campaign. Is it to increase website traffic, generate leads, or boost e-commerce sales?

.

.

KPI Selection: Based on the campaign objective, select relevant KPIs that will measure the campaign's success. For instance, if the goal is to increase website traffic, KPIs might include website sessions, bounce rate, and page views.

.

.

Benchmarking: Establish benchmark values or baseline metrics for each selected KPI. This provides a starting point for tracking progress.

.

.

Data Tracking Plan: Outline how you will collect and track data for the chosen KPIs, including the tools and analytics platforms you'll use.

.

.

Monitoring Strategy: Develop a strategy for regular monitoring and reporting on the selected KPIs throughout the campaign.

.

.

Performance Analysis: As the campaign progresses, analyze KPI data to assess whether the campaign is meeting its objectives and whether adjustments are needed.

.

Defining KPIs for a fictional client's campaign will help you understand the importance of aligning campaign goals with measurable metrics and how to use KPI data for optimization and reporting.

In the following chapters, we'll explore strategies for multi-channel marketing, remarketing, and client communication, all of which contribute to achieving and demonstrating a strong ROI in digital marketing.

☒

In this section, we will continue our exploration of measuring success and return on investment (ROI) by focusing on two essential elements: data analytics tools and conversion tracking. These tools and practices are instrumental in gathering and analyzing data to assess the effectiveness of your digital marketing campaigns.

6.2 Data Analytics Tools

Data analytics tools are the backbone of successful digital marketing campaigns. These tools help collect, process, and visualize data, enabling marketers to make informed decisions and optimize their strategies.

Key Elements of Data Analytics Tools:

.

Tool Selection: Choose the right data analytics tools based on your campaign's needs. Popular options include Google Analytics, Adobe Analytics, and social media analytics platforms.

.

.

Data Integration: Integrate various data sources into a centralized platform for a holistic view of campaign performance.

Custom Reporting: Create custom dashboards and reports tailored to your campaign objectives and key performance indicators (KPIs).

Data Visualization: Use data visualization techniques such as graphs, charts, and heatmaps to make data insights more accessible.

Data Security: Ensure data security and compliance with privacy regulations when handling sensitive customer information.

Why Data Analytics Tools Matter:

Informed Decision-Making: Data analytics tools provide the insights needed for data-driven decisions and campaign optimization.

Tracking Progress: These tools help track campaign progress in real-time, allowing for timely adjustments.

Performance Visualization: Visualizing data makes it easier to communicate insights to clients or team members.

Historical Data: Analyzing historical data can reveal trends and patterns that inform future strategies.

Real-Life Success Story:

Case Study: Netflix's Data-Driven Content Strategy

Netflix uses data analytics extensively to recommend content to its users and create original shows. Their data-driven approach contributed to the success of shows like "House of Cards" and "Stranger Things," as they were created based on insights about viewer preferences.

Real-Life Task: Utilize Data Analytics Tools

To gain practical experience in using data analytics tools, follow these steps:

Task: Utilize Data Analytics Tools for a Fictional Client's Campaign

Client Persona: Choose one of your fictional clients or create a new one for this task.

Tool Selection: Select a data analytics tool (e.g., Google Analytics) to use for monitoring and analyzing campaign data.

Data Integration: Ensure that all relevant data sources, such as website traffic, social media metrics, and email campaign data, are integrated into the chosen analytics tool.

Custom Reporting: Create a custom report or dashboard within the tool that focuses on the selected KPIs for the client's campaign.

Data Visualization: Use the tool's data visualization capabilities to create charts or graphs that provide a clear visual representation of campaign performance.

.

.

Data Security Measures: Implement data security measures to protect sensitive information and ensure compliance with data privacy regulations.

.

.

Analysis and Optimization: Regularly analyze the data within the tool and use the insights gained to optimize the campaign.

.

Utilizing data analytics tools for a fictional client's campaign will allow you to become proficient in collecting, analyzing, and visualizing data—a skill set crucial for demonstrating ROI and making data-driven decisions in digital marketing.

6.3 Conversion Tracking

Conversion tracking is the practice of monitoring and measuring the actions that users take on your website or digital channels, such as making a purchase or submitting a contact form. It is fundamental for understanding how effectively your campaigns are driving desired outcomes.

Key Elements of Conversion Tracking:

.

Conversion Goals: Define specific conversion goals that align with your campaign objectives, such as e-commerce purchases, lead form submissions, or newsletter sign-ups.

.

.

Conversion Tracking Codes: Implement conversion tracking codes (e.g., Google Ads conversion tracking) on your website to capture user interactions.

.

.

Attribution Modeling: Understand how different touchpoints contribute to conversions by using attribution modeling.

.

.

Multi-Channel Tracking: Track conversions across various digital channels and devices to gain a comprehensive view of user behavior.

.

.

Conversion Rate Optimization (CRO): Continuously work on improving the conversion rate by optimizing landing pages, forms, and CTAs.

.

Why Conversion Tracking Matters:

.

Performance Assessment: Conversion tracking allows you to assess how effectively your campaigns are driving desired actions.

Budget Allocation: It helps in allocating your budget to channels and campaigns that generate the highest conversions.

Campaign Optimization: Insights from conversion tracking inform campaign optimization strategies.

Client Reporting: Demonstrating the impact of conversions is vital for client reporting and showcasing ROI.

.

Real-Life Success Story:

Case Study: Dropbox's Referral Program

Dropbox's referral program, which allowed users to refer friends in exchange for additional storage space, was a conversion tracking success. They used conversion tracking to monitor and optimize the program, leading to rapid user growth.

Real-Life Task: Implement Conversion Tracking

To gain practical experience in implementing conversion tracking, follow these steps:

Task: Implement Conversion Tracking for a Fictional Client's Campaign

Client Persona: Choose one of your fictional clients or create a new one for this task.

Conversion Goals: Define specific conversion goals that align with the client's campaign objectives. For example, if it's an e-commerce campaign, the goal might be online purchases.

Conversion Tracking Codes: Set up conversion tracking codes or pixels within the chosen analytics or advertising platform (e.g., Google Ads, Faceb

Ads) to track the defined conversion goals.

Attribution Modeling: Explore attribution models within the platform to understand how different touchpoints contribute to conversions.

.

.

Multi-Channel Tracking: Ensure that conversion tracking spans across various digital channels and devices used by your audience.

.

Conversion Rate Optimization (CRO): As data accumulates, analyze the
conversion data to identify opportunities for improving the conversion rate. This may involve optimizing landing pages, forms, or ad creatives.

.

.

Performance Reporting: Create reports that showcase the conversion metrics, their impact on ROI, and the effectiveness of the campaign.

.

Implementing conversion tracking for a fictional client's campaign will equip you with hands-on experience in setting up tracking mechanisms, interpreting conversion data, and optimizing campaigns for better results.

In the upcoming chapters, we will delve into multi-channel marketing, remarketing strategies, and the importance of clear communication with clients to ensure they understand the value of your efforts in driving conversions and ROI.

Reporting to Clients and Continuous Improvement

We'll explore the crucial aspects of reporting campaign results to clients and the ongoing process of continuous improvement. These practices ensure transparency, client satisfaction, and the refinement of your digital marketing strategies.

6.4 Reporting to Clients

Effective communication with clients is essential for building trust and demonstrating the value of your digital marketing efforts. Regular, insightful reporting is a cornerstone of client-agency relationships.

Key Elements of Reporting to Clients:

.

Transparency: Provide clients with transparent, honest, and clear reports that align with their goals and objectives.

.

.

Key Performance Indicators (KPIs): Highlight KPIs that matter most to the client and show progress toward achieving their objectives.

.

.

Customization: Tailor reports to suit the client's preferences and level of detail they require.

.

.

Data Visualization: Use data visualization techniques like charts and graphs to make data more accessible and understandable.

.

.

Insights and Recommendations: Offer insights derived from data analysis and provide actionable recommendations for optimization.

.

Why Reporting to Clients Matters:

.

Client Satisfaction: Transparent reporting fosters trust and keeps clients informed and satisfied.

Data-Driven Decisions: Reports provide the data needed for clients to make informed decisions about their digital marketing strategies.

Accountability: Reports hold both the agency and the client accountable for agreed-upon goals and objectives.

Budget Allocation: Clients can use reports to evaluate the allocation of their marketing budget.

.

Real-Life Success Story:

Case Study: Moz's Transparent Reporting

Moz, a well-known SEO software company, has gained a reputation for transparent reporting. They share their successes and failures openly with clients, emphasizing the importance of transparency in building long-term partnerships.

Real-Life Task: Create a Client Report

To gain hands-on experience in creating client reports, follow these steps:

Task: Create a Client Report for a Fictional Client's Digital Marketing Campaign

- **Client Persona:** Choose one of your fictional clients or create a new one for this task.

- **Report Template:** Select or create a report template that suits the client's preferences and the campaign's objectives.

- **Data Compilation:** Gather relevant campaign data, including KPIs, analytics, and performance metrics.

- **Data Visualization:** Use data visualization tools or software to create visually appealing charts and graphs.

- **Insights and Recommendations:** Analyze the data and derive insights. Provide actionable recommendations for optimizing the campaign.

- **Client Presentation:** If applicable, prepare to present the report to the client, either in person or via a video conference.

- **Feedback and Discussion:** Encourage the client to ask questions, provide feedback, and engage in a discussion about the campaign's performance.

Creating a client report for a fictional client will allow you to develop the skills needed for transparent and effective reporting in real client-agency relationships.

6.5 Continuous Improvement

Continuous improvement is an ongoing process of refining and enhancing your digital marketing strategies. It involves learning from past campaigns, staying updated on industry trends, and adapting to changes in the digital landscape.

Key Elements of Continuous Improvement:

.

Campaign Debriefs: Conduct post-campaign debriefs to analyze what worked, what didn't, and what can be improved.

.

.

Competitive Analysis: Continually assess competitors' strategies and learn from their successes and failures.

.

.

Industry Updates: Stay informed about industry trends, algorithm changes, and emerging technologies.

.

.

Training and Skill Development: Invest in ongoing training to keep your team's skills up-to-date.

.

.

Client Feedback: Act on client feedback and make adjustments based on their input.

.

Why Continuous Improvement Matters:

.

Staying Relevant: In the fast-paced digital landscape, staying relevant is crucial for success.

Optimizing ROI: Continuous improvement helps optimize campaign performance and ROI.

Client Satisfaction: Clients appreciate agencies that are proactive in refining their strategies.

Learning from Mistakes: It allows you to learn from past mistakes and avoid repeating them.

.

Real-Life Success Story:

Case Study: Google's Algorithm Updates

Google continuously updates its search algorithms to provide users with better results. Digital marketers who stay updated on these changes and adapt their strategies accordingly are more likely to maintain high search rankings and traffic.

Real-Life Task: Create a Continuous Improvement Plan

To gain practical experience in creating a continuous improvement plan, follow these steps:

Task: Develop a Continuous Improvement Plan for a Fictional Client's Digital Marketing Campaign

.

Client Persona: Choose one of your fictional clients or create a new one for this task.

.

.

Campaign Assessment: Review the performance of a previous campaign for this client.

.

.

Identify Areas for Improvement: Based on the assessment, identify areas within the campaign that need improvement. This could include targeting, messaging, or channel selection.

.

.

Competitive Analysis: Research and analyze the strategies of competitors in the client's industry.

.

.

Industry Trends: Stay updated on industry trends and changes in algorithms or platform policies that could impact your strategies.

.

.

Skill Development: Identify any skills or knowledge gaps within your team and plan for training or skill development.

.

.

Client Feedback: Collect feedback from the client about their satisfaction with the previous campaign and any suggestions for improvement.

.

.

Continuous Improvement Plan: Create a plan that outlines specific actions and strategies for continuous improvement in the upcoming campaign.

.

Developing a continuous improvement plan for a fictional client will help you understand the importance of learning from past campaigns, adapting to industry changes, and continuously enhancing your digital marketing strategies.

In the upcoming chapters, we will delve into multi-channel marketing, remarketing strategies, and client communication best practices to ensure you are well-equipped for successful digital marketing agency operations.

Chapter Seven

Challenges and Pitfalls

In this chapter, we will explore the various challenges and pitfalls that digital marketing agencies may encounter in their operations. Learning from common mistakes and knowing how to avoid them is crucial for maintaining client satisfaction and achieving success.

7.1 Common Mistakes to Avoid

Overlooking Mobile Optimization

Challenge: Neglecting mobile optimization is a common mistake that can significantly hinder campaign performance. With the increasing use of smartphones, ensuring that your digital assets are mobile-friendly is essential.

Real-Life Task: Mobile Optimization Audit

To address the challenge of mobile optimization, conduct a mobile optimization audit for a fictional client's website:

Task: Mobile Optimization Audit for a Fictional Client's Website

- **Client Persona:** Choose one of your fictional clients or create a new one for this task.

- **Website Evaluation:** Assess the client's website for mobile optimization, including page load speed, responsive design, and user experience on mobile devices.

- **Recommendations:** Based on your evaluation, provide recommendations for optimizing the website for mobile users. This may include responsive design adjustments, image optimization, and mobile-specific content improvements.

- **Testing:** Test the recommended changes to ensure they enhance the mobile user experience.

- **Reporting:** Prepare a brief report outlining your findings and recommendations for the client.

Addressing mobile optimization challenges ensures that your campaigns reach a broader audience and provide a better user experience across devices.

Neglecting Content Quality

Challenge: Focusing solely on content quantity rather than quality is a mistake that can lead to decreased engagement and conversion rates. High-quality, valuable content is essential for attracting and retaining an audience.

Real-Life Task: Content Quality Assessment

To tackle the challenge of neglecting content quality, conduct a content quality assessment for a fictional client's blog:

Task: Content Quality Assessment for a Fictional Client's Blog

Client Persona: Choose one of your fictional clients or create a new one for this task.

Blog Evaluation: Review the client's blog posts, considering factors such as relevance, depth of information, writing style, and engagement metrics (e.g., comments, shares).

Quality Scoring: Develop a scoring system or checklist to assess the quality of each blog post objectively.

Recommendations: Based on your assessment, provide

recommendations for improving the quality of future blog posts. This may involve topic selection, research depth, and storytelling techniques.

.

.

Content Calendar: Work with the client to create a content calendar that prioritizes quality over quantity.

.

.

Measuring Improvement: After implementing changes, measure the impact on engagement metrics and conversion rates.

.

Emphasizing content quality in your campaigns ensures that your audience finds value in your content, leading to increased brand trust and customer loyalty.

Inadequate Budget Allocation

Challenge: Allocating an inadequate budget to digital marketing campaigns can limit their effectiveness. It's essential to strike a balance between cost-effectiveness and budget sufficiency.

Real-Life Task: Budget Optimization

To address the challenge of inadequate budget allocation, optimize the budget for a fictional client's social media advertising campaign:

Task: Budget Optimization for a Fictional Client's Social Media Advertising Campaign

.

Client Persona: Choose one of your fictional clients or create a new one for this task.

.

.

Campaign Evaluation: Review the client's social media advertising campaign, including ad spend, ad performance, and conversion rates.

.

.

Budget Reallocation: Based on your evaluation, reallocate the budget to prioritize high-performing ad sets and channels while reducing spending on less effective ones.

.

.

Testing: Implement the budget changes and closely monitor their impact on campaign performance.

.

.

Performance Reporting: Create a report showcasing the impact of budget optimization on key performance indicators, such as return on ad spend (ROAS) or cost per conversion.

.

Optimizing budget allocation ensures that you get the most out of your marketing budget and achieve a higher ROI for your clients.

Real-Life Success Story:

Case Study: Airbnb's Mobile Optimization

Airbnb recognized the importance of mobile optimization and invested in improving its mobile app and website experience. As a result, mobile bookings increased significantly, contributing to the company's success.

Learning from common challenges and avoiding these pitfalls is vital for digital marketing agencies. In the next chapters, we will explore advanced strategies, multi-channel marketing, and client communication techniques to further enhance your agency's capabilities and client satisfaction.

Dealing with Algorithm Changes and Managing Client Expectations

7.2 Dealing with Algorithm Changes

Challenge: The digital landscape is ever-evolving, with search engines and social media platforms frequently updating their algorithms. Adapting to these changes is crucial for maintaining campaign effectiveness.

Real-Life Task: Algorithm Change Adaptation

To address the challenge of dealing with algorithm changes, simulate an algorithm update scenario for a fictional client's SEO campaign:

Task: Algorithm Change Adaptation for a Fictional Client's SEO Campaign

- **Client Persona:** Choose one of your fictional clients or create a new one for this task.

- **Algorithm Update Simulation:** Create a fictional algorithm update that impacts your client's industry or niche. Consider changes related to ranking factors, content quality, or user experience.

-

Assessment: Analyze the client's website and SEO strategy to identify potential areas of concern or non-compliance with the simulated algorithm changes.

-

Adjustment Plan: Develop a plan to adapt the client's SEO strategy to align with the simulated algorithm update. This may involve content revisions, technical SEO improvements, or backlink audits.

-

Implementation: Execute the adjustments and closely monitor the campaign's performance after the simulated algorithm update.

-

Performance Report: Prepare a performance report detailing the impact of the algorithm change and the effectiveness of your adaptation strategy.

-

By practicing adaptation to algorithm changes, you'll be better equipped to handle real-world updates that may affect your clients' campaigns.

7.3 Managing Client Expectations

Challenge: Clients often have high expectations for digital marketing outcomes, which can lead to dissatisfaction if not properly managed. Effective communication and setting realistic expectations are essential.

Real-Life Task: Setting Expectations

To tackle the challenge of managing client expectations, create a client expectation-setting plan for a fictional client:

Task: Client Expectation-Setting Plan for a Fictional Client

.

Client Persona: Choose one of your fictional clients or create a new one for this task.

.

.

Client Assessment: Assess the client's goals, objectives, and prior expectations regarding campaign performance.

.

.

Realistic Expectations: Based on your assessment, set realistic and achievable expectations for the upcoming campaign. Ensure that these expectations are in line with industry benchmarks and historical data.

.

.

Communication Plan: Develop a communication plan that outlines how you will convey these expectations to the client effectively.

.

.

Feedback Loop: Establish a feedback loop with the client to ensure ongoing alignment of expectations throughout the campaign.

.

.

Education: Educate the client about the dynamic nature of digital marketing, emphasizing that results may vary over time due to various factors.

Real-Life Success Story:

Case Study: HubSpot's Content Strategy

HubSpot's content marketing strategy emphasizes the importance of managing client expectations through educational content. By providing resources that explain the realities of digital marketing, they set realistic expectations and build trust with clients.

Effectively dealing with algorithm changes and managing client expectations are critical skills for digital marketing agencies. In the following chapters, we will explore advanced strategies for multi-channel marketing, client retention, and scaling your agency's operations.

7.4 Handling Negative Reviews and Feedback

In this chapter, we'll delve into the challenging but essential task of managing negative reviews and feedback in the digital marketing world. Negative feedback can be an opportunity for growth and improvement when handled effectively.

The Importance of Addressing Negative Reviews

Challenge: Negative reviews and feedback can impact a business's reputation and influence potential customers' decisions. Ignoring or mishandling them can be detrimental.

Real-Life Task: Negative Review Resolution

To address the challenge of handling negative reviews, create a plan to resolve a fictional client's negative online reviews:

Task: Negative Review Resolution Plan for a Fictional Client

.

Client Persona: Choose one of your fictional clients or create a new one for
this task.

.

.

Review Assessment: Identify negative reviews and feedback related to the client's business, products, or services.

.

.

Review Analysis: Categorize negative reviews based on common themes or issues. Determine the severity of each review.

.

.

Resolution Strategy: Develop a strategy for addressing each category of negative reviews, including response templates, possible solutions, and escalation procedures if needed.

.

.

Response Guidelines: Establish guidelines for responding to negative reviews professionally, empathetically, and constructively. Addressing concerns and proposing solutions can help turn negative experiences into positive ones.

.

.

Monitoring and Follow-Up: Implement a system for monitoring review platforms and promptly addressing new negative reviews. Follow up with customers to ensure their concerns have been resolved.

.

Real-Life Success Story:

Case Study: Airbnb's Response to Trust and Safety Concerns

Airbnb faced challenges related to trust and safety after a few high-profile incidents. They implemented robust safety measures and improved their customer support system to address negative feedback. Their proactive approach helped rebuild trust among their user base.

Effectively handling negative reviews can not only mitigate potential damage but also demonstrate your commitment to customer satisfaction and continuous improvement.

Leveraging Negative Feedback for Improvement

Challenge: Negative feedback, when viewed as constructive criticism, can be a valuable resource for improvement. However, this perspective shift can be challenging.

Real-Life Task: Feedback Integration

To address the challenge of leveraging negative feedback for improvement, create a plan for integrating feedback into a fictional client's digital marketing strategy:

Task: Feedback Integration Plan for a Fictional Client

.

Client Persona: Choose one of your fictional clients or create a new one for this task.

.

.

Feedback Collection: Gather feedback from various sources, including customer reviews, surveys, and social media comments.

.

.

Feedback Analysis: Analyze the feedback to identify recurring themes, pain points, and areas of improvement.

.

.

Priority Setting: Prioritize the feedback based on its potential impact on the client's business objectives and customer satisfaction.

.

.

Integration Plan: Develop a plan to integrate feedback-driven improvements into the client's digital marketing strategy. This may involve website enhancements, product/service updates, or changes to marketing messaging.

.

.

Testing and Optimization: Implement the planned improvements and continuously test and optimize to ensure they have the desired impact.

.

By actively seeking and implementing feedback-driven improvements, you can demonstrate your commitment to excellence and adaptability as a digital marketing agency.

Real-Life Success Story:

Case Study: Amazon's Customer Feedback Integration

Amazon consistently leverages customer feedback to enhance

its e-commerce platform. Customer reviews and feedback have led to product improvements, enhanced customer support, and a better overall shopping experience.

Effectively handling negative reviews and feedback, and turning them into opportunities for improvement, is a hallmark of a customer-centric approach in digital marketing.

In the following chapters, we will explore advanced strategies for managing multi-channel marketing campaigns, client retention, and scaling your agency's operations to achieve even greater success in the digital marketing world.

Chapter Eight

Staying Current in a Dynamic Industry - Industry Trends and Updates

In this chapter, we'll explore the importance of staying current with industry trends and updates in the dynamic field of digital marketing. Keeping abreast of changes is vital for offering clients the latest strategies and maintaining a competitive edge.

The Necessity of Staying Current

Challenge: Digital marketing is in a constant state of evolution. New platforms, algorithms, and consumer behaviors emerge regularly. Failing to stay current can result in outdated strategies and diminished campaign performance.

8.1 Real-Life Task: Industry Trend Analysis

To address the challenge of staying current with industry trends, create a plan to analyze trends and updates for a fictional client's industry:

Task: Industry Trend Analysis Plan for a Fictional Client

- **Client Persona:** Choose one of your fictional clients or create a new one for this task.

Trend Identification: Identify the client's industry and niche, and research recent trends, innovations, and updates relevant to that industry.

-
-

Competitor Analysis: Analyze the digital marketing strategies of competitors within the same industry, focusing on successful approaches and emerging trends.

-
-

Client Impact Assessment: Determine how these trends and updates could potentially impact your client's digital marketing strategy, from content creation to advertising channels.

-
-

Integration Plan: Develop a plan for integrating relevant trends and updates into your client's digital marketing strategy. This may involve adjustments to content calendars, SEO strategies, or ad campaigns.

-
-

Reporting and Monitoring: Establish a system for continuous monitoring of industry trends and competitor strategies and reporting relevant insights to your client.

-

Real-Life Success Story:

Case Study: Nike's Agile Response to Market Trends

Nike, a global leader in sportswear, stays current with industry trends by closely monitoring consumer behavior and emerging technologies. They were quick to embrace e-commerce trends and adapt their marketing strategies accordingly, resulting in significant growth in online sales.

By staying current with industry trends, you can position your agency as an industry leader and offer clients strategies that are both effective and forward-thinking.

Embracing Emerging Technologies

Challenge: Emerging technologies, such as artificial intelligence (AI), augmented reality (AR), and voice search, are transforming the digital marketing landscape. Failing to adopt these technologies can leave your agency at a disadvantage.

Real-Life Task: Technology Integration

To address the challenge of embracing emerging technologies, create a plan for integrating one of these technologies into a fictional client's digital marketing strategy:

Task: Emerging Technology Integration Plan for a Fictional Client

- **Client Persona:** Choose one of your fictional clients or create a new one for this task.

- **Technology Selection:** Select an emerging technology (e.g., AI chatbots, voice search optimization, or AR advertising) relevant to the client's industry.

- **Assessment:** Evaluate how the selected technology can enhance the client's digital marketing efforts, such as improving user experience or personalizing content.

- .
- .

Implementation Plan: Develop a step-by-step plan for integrating the technology, including resource allocation, technology acquisition, and training.

- .
- .

Testing and Optimization: Implement the technology and conduct thorough testing to ensure it functions effectively. Optimize its use based on performance data.

- .
- .

Results Reporting: Create a report showcasing the impact of the technology integration on key performance indicators (KPIs) and user engagement.

- .

Real-Life Success Story:

Case Study: Starbucks' Use of AI for Personalization

Starbucks utilizes AI technology to personalize its app, offering tailored recommendations and rewards to customers. This approach significantly increased user engagement and sales through the app.

Embracing emerging technologies not only improves campaign effectiveness but also demonstrates your agency's commitment to innovation and client success.

In the following chapters, we will explore advanced strategies for managing multi-channel marketing campaigns, client retention, and scaling your agency's operations for continued growth and success in the digital marketing industry.

We'll dive into two critical aspects of running a successful digital marketing agency: navigating algorithm changes and effectively managing client expectations. Staying adaptable and ensuring clients understand the dynamic nature of digital marketing are key to long-term success.

8.2 Continuous Learning and Professional Development -

Networking and Collaboration

We'll explore the critical importance of continuous learning and professional development in the ever-evolving field of digital marketing. Additionally, we'll delve into the power of networking and collaboration as means to enhance your agency's capabilities and opportunities for growth.

Continuous Learning and Professional Development

Challenge: Digital marketing is a field that undergoes constant transformation. Keeping your skills and knowledge up-to-date is essential to remain competitive and deliver the best possible results for clients.

Real-Life Task: Continuous Learning Plan

To address the challenge of continuous learning and professional development, create a plan for enhancing your team's skills:

Task: Continuous Learning Plan for Your Digital Marketing Team

Skills Assessment: Assess the current skillset of your team members and identify areas where improvement is needed.

Training Opportunities: Research relevant training programs, online courses, workshops, and certifications that align with the identified skill gaps.

Individual Learning Plans: Develop individualized learning plans for each team member, outlining the courses or resources they should engage with, and set realistic goals for skill development.

Implementation: Allocate time and resources for team members to pursue their individual learning plans. Encourage knowledge-sharing and collaboration among team members.

Monitoring Progress: Regularly check in with team members to gauge their progress and provide support as needed.

Integration into Campaigns: Implement the newly acquired knowledge and skills into your agency's digital marketing campaigns.

Real-Life Success Story:

Case Study: HubSpot Academy's Impact on Digital Marketing

HubSpot offers a comprehensive range of free online courses and certifications through HubSpot Academy. Many digital marketers have benefited from these resources, improving their skills and applying newfound knowledge to their campaigns effectively.

Continuous learning is not only a personal growth strategy but also an investment in the success of your agency and its clients.

8.3 Networking and Collaboration

Challenge: In digital marketing, networking and collaboration can open doors to new opportunities, partnerships, and insights. However, building a robust professional network and fostering collaboration can be challenging.

Real-Life Task: Networking and Collaboration Strategy

To address the challenge of networking and collaboration, create a strategy for expanding your agency's professional network:

Task: Networking and Collaboration Strategy for Your Digital Marketing Agency

Targeted Networking: Identify industry-specific events, conferences, webinars, and online communities relevant to digital marketing. Select the ones that align with your agency's goals and objectives.

Team Involvement: Encourage team members to actively participate in networking opportunities, whether through attending events, joining online forums, or engaging with industry thought leaders on social media.

- **Partnership Exploration:** Explore potential partnerships with complementary businesses or agencies. Collaborative projects can expand your service offerings and reach.

- **Content Collaboration:** Seek opportunities to collaborate on content creation with other professionals in your field. Guest posting, podcast interviews, and joint webinars can enhance your agency's visibility.

- **Client Referrals:** Develop a client referral program to incentivize clients to refer your agency to others in their network.

- **Metrics for Success:** Define key performance indicators (KPIs) for your networking and collaboration efforts, such as the number of new connections made or the revenue generated from partnerships.

Real-Life Success Story:

Case Study: Neil Patel's Collaborative Content Strategy

Digital marketing expert Neil Patel has built a vast network of collaborators in the industry. He frequently engages in collaborative content projects, such as webinars and podcast interviews, which have contributed to his thought leadership and agency's success.

Networking and collaboration are invaluable tools for expanding your agency's reach, gaining insights from peers, and discovering new business opportunities.

In the following chapters, we will explore advanced strategies for managing multi-channel marketing campaigns, client retention, and scaling your agency's operations for continued growth and success in the dynamic field of digital marketing.

8.4 Adapting to Technological Advancements

We'll explore the vital role of adapting to technological advancements in the digital marketing landscape. Staying ahead of the curve in technology can significantly impact your agency's success.

The Impact of Technological Advancements

Challenge: Rapid technological advancements can disrupt the digital marketing industry and change the way campaigns are executed and measured. Adapting to these changes is crucial for maintaining competitiveness.

Real-Life Task: Technology Adoption Strategy

To address the challenge of adapting to technological advancements, create a strategy for adopting a new technology relevant to digital marketing:

Task: Technology Adoption Strategy for Your Digital Marketing Agency

Technology Selection: Identify a specific technology or tool that has recently emerged and has the potential to improve your agency's digital marketing capabilities.

-
-

Assessment: Evaluate how this technology aligns with your agency's goals and objectives. Determine its potential impact on campaign performance and efficiency.

-
-

Pilot Implementation: Implement the technology on a smaller scale or in a controlled environment, such as a single campaign or project.

-
-

Testing and Optimization: Gather data during the pilot implementation to assess the technology's effectiveness. Make necessary adjustments and optimizations.

-
-

Full Integration: If the technology proves successful during the pilot phase, roll it out across your agency's operations. Provide training and support to your team for seamless integration.

-
-

Monitoring and Evaluation: Continuously monitor the technology's performance and gather feedback from your team. Be prepared to pivot if the technology's effectiveness wanes or if better alternatives emerge.

-

Real-Life Success Story:

Case Study: Spotify's Use of Machine Learning for Personalized Playlists

Spotify utilizes machine learning algorithms to create

personalized playlists for users. This technology-driven approach has significantly increased user engagement and satisfaction.

Adapting to technological advancements can not only enhance your agency's capabilities but also demonstrate your commitment to delivering innovative solutions to clients.

Chapter Nine

Scaling Your Digital Marketing Agency - Scaling Strategies

In this chapter, we will explore essential strategies for scaling your digital marketing agency, allowing you to expand your operations, reach a broader client base, and achieve sustainable growth.

9.1 The Need for Scaling Strategies

Challenge: As your agency grows, it becomes increasingly important to implement effective scaling strategies to accommodate more clients, deliver high-quality services, and maintain profitability.

Real-Life Task: Scaling Plan

To address the challenge of scaling your agency, create a plan outlining how you will scale your operations while maintaining service quality:

Task: Scaling Plan for Your Digital Marketing Agency

- **Assessment:** Conduct a thorough assessment of your agency's current capacity, including staff, technology, and resources.

- **Client Segmentation:** Segment your clients based on their needs, budgets, and the services they require.

- **Service Packages:** Create standardized service packages tailored to different client segments, ensuring scalability and profitability.

-
-

Staffing Strategy: Evaluate your staffing needs and consider options such as hiring additional team members, outsourcing specific tasks, or implementing automation solutions.

-
-

Technology Integration: Identify technology solutions that can streamline your agency's processes and improve efficiency, such as project management tools or marketing automation platforms.

-
-

Quality Control: Implement quality control measures to ensure that as your agency scales, the quality of services remains consistent.

-

Real-Life Success Story:

Case Study: HubSpot's Growth Through Inbound Marketing

HubSpot utilized inbound marketing strategies to attract clients and grew from a startup to a global digital marketing powerhouse. Their focus on providing valuable content and tailored services allowed them to scale while maintaining a high level of service quality.

Effective scaling strategies are essential for achieving sustainable growth and success in the digital marketing industry.

Leveraging Strategic Partnerships

Challenge: Building strategic partnerships can open up new opportunities for your agency, but identifying and nurturing these partnerships can be challenging.

Real-Life Task: Partnership Development

To address the challenge of leveraging strategic partnerships, create a plan to identify and nurture potential partnerships:

Task: Partnership Development Plan for Your Digital Marketing Agency

.

Identification: Identify potential strategic partners within the digital marketing ecosystem, such as web development agencies, content creators, or social media influencers.

.

.

Assessment: Evaluate the compatibility of potential partners based on their expertise, client base, and goals.

.

.

Value Proposition: Develop a clear value proposition that highlights the benefits of partnering with your agency, emphasizing how it can enhance the partner's offerings or reach.

.

.

Outreach: Reach out to potential partners through personalized communication, emphasizing the mutual advantages of collaboration.

.

.

Negotiation: Collaboratively define the terms of the partnership, including the scope of collaboration, revenue sharing, and shared responsibilities.

.

.

Execution: Implement the partnership agreement and ensure that both parties are aligned in delivering value to clients.

.

Real-Life Success Story:

Case Study: Hootsuite's Partner Program

Hootsuite, a social media management platform, has a robust partner program that enables agencies to offer social media services to their clients. By partnering with digital marketing agencies, Hootsuite has expanded its reach and provided agencies with valuable tools.

Strategic partnerships can help your agency access new clients, expertise, and resources, contributing to your growth and success.

In the following chapters, we will explore advanced strategies for managing multi-channel marketing campaigns, client retention, and maintaining excellence as you continue to scale your agency in the dynamic field of digital marketing.

Data Privacy and Ethical Considerations

Challenge: With the rise of data-driven marketing, concerns about data privacy and ethical considerations have grown. Navigating these issues is crucial to maintaining trust with clients and consumers.

Real-Life Task: Data Privacy Compliance

To address the challenge of data privacy and ethical considerations, create a plan to ensure your agency complies with relevant regulations:

Task: Data Privacy Compliance Plan for Your Digital Marketing Agency

Regulatory Assessment: Identify the data privacy regulations that apply to your agency and its clients. This may include GDPR, CCPA, or industry-specific regulations.

Data Audit: Conduct a comprehensive audit of the data you collect, store, and process. Identify sensitive data and ensure it is handled securely.

Privacy Policies: Review and update your agency's privacy policies to clearly communicate how data is collected, used, and protected.

Consent Mechanisms: Implement robust consent mechanisms for data collection and processing. Ensure that users have the option to opt in or opt out.

Data Security Measures: Enhance data security measures to protect against breaches and unauthorized access. Implement encryption and secure storage solutions.

.

Training and Awareness: Educate your team on data privacy regulations and best practices. Foster a culture of data ethics within your agency.

.

Real-Life Success Story:

Case Study: Apple's Emphasis on User Privacy

Apple has prioritized user privacy by implementing features such as App Tracking Transparency (ATT), which allows users to control app tracking. This approach has resonated with consumers and strengthened Apple's brand.

Addressing data privacy and ethical considerations not only ensures compliance but also fosters trust and credibility, which are vital in the digital marketing industry.

In the session we will explore advanced strategies for managing multi-channel marketing campaigns, client retention, and scaling your agency's operations for continued growth and success in the dynamic field of digital marketing.

Managing Multi-Channel Marketing Campaigns

In this chapter, we will delve into the complexities of managing multi-channel marketing campaigns. Successfully orchestrating campaigns across various channels requires a strategic approach, effective coordination, and a deep understanding of each channel's unique characteristics.

The Challenge of Multi-Channel Marketing

Challenge: As digital marketing evolves, the need to engage with audiences across multiple channels has become imperative. Managing campaigns across various channels presents challenges related to coordination, consistency, and optimization.

Real-Life Task: Multi-Channel Campaign Strategy

To address the challenge of managing multi-channel marketing campaigns, create a comprehensive strategy for your agency:

Task: Multi-Channel Campaign Strategy for Your Digital Marketing Agency

Channel Selection: Identify the most relevant channels for your client's goals, considering factors such as target audience, industry, and budget.

Content Planning: Develop a content strategy that aligns with each channel's requirements and audience preferences. Ensure consistency in messaging and branding across channels.

Campaign Calendar: Create a campaign calendar that outlines the timing, frequency, and goals of each campaign on every chosen channel.

Cross-Channel Coordination: Implement tools or processes for seamless coordination between team members responsible for different channels.

Data Integration: Establish a system for collecting and

analyzing data from various channels to gain insights into campaign performance and audience behavior.

.

.

Optimization Strategy: Regularly review campaign performance data and adjust strategies based on what works best for each channel.

.

Real-Life Success Story:

Case Study: Coca-Cola's "Share a Coke" Campaign

Coca-Cola's "Share a Coke" campaign was a multi-channel success. It involved personalizing Coca-Cola bottles with people's names and encouraging consumers to share their experiences on social media. The campaign ran across TV, social media, print, and in-store promotions, demonstrating the power of multi-channel marketing.

Successfully managing multi-channel marketing campaigns requires a well-structured strategy and the ability to adapt to the unique dynamics of each channel.

Client Retention in Multi-Channel Campaigns

Challenge: Maintaining client satisfaction and retention in the context of multi-channel campaigns can be challenging due to the complexity of coordinating efforts and demonstrating the value of each channel.

Real-Life Task: Client Retention Plan

To address the challenge of client retention in multi-channel campaigns, develop a plan that focuses on client satisfaction and ongoing value delivery:

Task: Client Retention Plan for Your Digital Marketing Agency

.

Client Education: Educate your clients about the benefits and challenges of multi-channel marketing. Set realistic expectations for campaign outcomes.

.

.

Transparent Reporting: Provide clients with regular, transparent reports that highlight the performance of each channel and its contribution to their overall goals.

.

.

Communication: Maintain open and frequent communication with clients. Address their concerns promptly and provide proactive recommendations for campaign improvements.

.

.

Performance Reviews: Conduct periodic performance reviews with clients to assess the effectiveness of each channel and make necessary adjustments.

.

.

Testing and Optimization: Continuously test and optimize campaigns to maximize results and demonstrate your commitment to delivering value.

.

.

Feedback Loop: Encourage clients to provide feedback on their experience with your agency and use their input to enhance your services.

.

Real-Life Success Story:

Case Study: Google Ads Agency's Client Retention

A Google Ads agency successfully retained clients by providing regular reports that detailed the impact of each Google Ads campaign on lead generation and conversion rates. The agency's transparency and commitment to optimizing campaigns resulted in long-term client relationships.

Client retention is a vital component of agency success, especially in the context of multi-channel campaigns where ongoing communication and value demonstration are key.

In the following chapters, we will explore advanced strategies for maintaining excellence as you continue to scale your agency and navigate the dynamic field of digital marketing.

Chapter Ten

Case Studies and Success Stories - Real-Life Examples of Digital Marketing Campaigns

In this chapter, we will delve into real-life case studies and success stories of digital marketing campaigns. These examples will showcase the power of strategic planning, creativity, and effective execution in achieving outstanding results for clients. By studying these cases, you can gain valuable insights and inspiration for your own digital marketing campaigns.

10.1 Case Study: Airbnb's "Live There" Campaign

Background: Airbnb, a global online marketplace for lodging and travel experiences, faced stiff competition and a need to differentiate itself from traditional hotels. They aimed to emphasize the unique experiences offered by hosts to travelers.

Strategy: Airbnb launched the "Live There" campaign, highlighting the idea that when you stay with Airbnb, you don't just visit a place; you live there. They focused on user-generated content, showcasing real hosts and travelers sharing their experiences.

Results:

Real-Life Task: Campaign Strategy Assessment

Task: Analyze the "Live There" campaign and identify key elements that contributed to its success. Consider how you can apply similar strategies, such as user-generated content and authentic storytelling, to your own campaigns.

10.2 Case Study: Dove's "Real Beauty" Campaign

Background: Dove, a personal care brand, aimed to challenge beauty stereotypes and promote real beauty in advertising. They sought to empower women to feel confident in their own skin.

Strategy: Dove's "Real Beauty" campaign featured real women of diverse ages and body types in their advertisements. They conducted a study on self-esteem and launched the Dove Self-Esteem Project to support women and girls.

Results:

Real-Life Task: Embracing Authenticity

Task: Explore how you can infuse authenticity and inclusivity into your digital marketing campaigns. Consider the impact of showcasing real people and addressing relevant social issues.

10.3 Case Study: Nike's "Just Do It" Campaign with Colin Kaepernick

Background: Nike, a leading sports apparel brand, faced controversy when they featured former NFL quarterback Colin Kaepernick in their "Just Do It" campaign. Kaepernick is known for his protests against racial injustice during the national anthem.

Strategy: Nike took a bold stance by featuring Kaepernick in an ad with the tagline "Believe in something. Even if it means sacrificing everything." The campaign aimed to align the brand with social justice movements and appeal to a younger, socially conscious audience.

Results:

Real-Life Task: Calculated Risk-Taking

Task: Reflect on the Nike campaign and consider how calculated risks and taking a stand on social issues can resonate with your target audience. Explore opportunities to align your brand with relevant causes.

10.4 Case Study: Red Bull's Content Marketing

Background: Red Bull, an energy drink company, sought to establish itself as a lifestyle brand associated with extreme sports, adventure, and excitement.

Strategy: Red Bull embraced content marketing by producing high-quality videos and articles showcasing extreme sports, events, and athletes. They created the Red Bull Media House to produce and distribute content across various channels.

Results:

Real-Life Task: Content Marketing Strategy

Task: Explore the power of content marketing and how you can create engaging, shareable content that aligns with your brand's identity. Consider how storytelling and multimedia can elevate your campaigns.

These case studies exemplify the transformative impact of effective digital marketing strategies. By studying these real-life examples, you can gain valuable insights into what makes campaigns successful and how you can apply similar principles to your own marketing endeavors.

In the final chapter of this guide, we will conclude our exploration of digital marketing and leave you with reflections on your journey and the ongoing pursuit of excellence in this dynamic field.

Chapter Eleven

Future of Digital Marketing Agencies - Predictions and Trends

In this chapter, we'll explore the exciting and evolving landscape of digital marketing agencies. The digital marketing industry is ever-changing, driven by technological advancements, shifts in consumer behavior, and emerging trends. By examining predictions and trends, you can position your agency for future success and innovation.

Prediction: Artificial Intelligence (AI) Integration

What to Expect: AI and machine learning will become integral to digital marketing. AI algorithms will refine targeting, personalize content, and optimize campaigns in real time.

Real-Life Task: AI Implementation

Task: Explore AI tools and platforms that can enhance your agency's capabilities. Consider how AI can improve audience targeting, content recommendations, and campaign optimization.

Trend: Voice Search Optimization

What to Expect: With the increasing use of voice-activated devices and voice search, optimizing content for voice queries will become essential. Agencies must adapt to voice search trends for their clients.

Real-Life Task: Voice Search Strategy

Task: Develop a voice search optimization strategy for your agency and clients. Consider how conversational keywords and structured data can enhance voice search visibility.

Prediction: Video Dominance

What to Expect: Video content will continue to dominate digital marketing. Short-form videos, live streaming, and interactive videos will be key components of successful campaigns.

Real-Life Task: Video Content Creation

Task: Invest in video content creation capabilities within your agency. Experiment with different video formats, such as live streams and interactive videos, to engage audiences effectively.

Trend: Privacy and Data Protection

What to Expect: Data privacy concerns will continue to shape digital marketing. Agencies must prioritize data protection and transparency in their strategies.

Real-Life Task: Data Privacy Compliance

Task: Stay informed about evolving data protection regulations and ensure your agency and clients are in compliance. Transparency in data collection and usage is crucial.

Prediction: Omni-Channel Marketing

What to Expect: Omni-channel marketing, which integrates various channels seamlessly, will become the norm. Agencies must deliver consistent messaging across all touchpoints.

Real-Life Task: Omni-Channel Strategy

Task: Develop an omni-channel marketing strategy for your agency and clients. Focus on delivering a unified brand experience across websites, social media, email, and more.

Trend: Sustainability and Social Responsibility

What to Expect: Consumers are increasingly valuing brands that demonstrate social responsibility and sustainability. Agencies should consider the environmental and ethical impact of their campaigns.

Real-Life Task: Sustainable Marketing

Task: Integrate sustainability and social responsibility into your agency's campaigns. Highlight clients' eco-friendly initiatives and ethical practices in marketing efforts.

Prediction: Augmented Reality (AR) and Virtual Reality (VR)

What to Expect: AR and VR technologies will play a larger role in marketing. Interactive AR ads and immersive VR experiences will offer new avenues for engagement.

Real-Life Task: AR and VR Experiences

Task: Explore how AR and VR can enhance your agency's campaigns. Experiment with creating interactive AR ads or immersive VR content.

Trend: Localized and Personalized Content

What to Expect: Consumers crave personalized experiences, including locally relevant content. Agencies should tailor content to specific regions and audiences.

Real-Life Task: Localized Marketing

Task: Incorporate localized and personalized content strategies into your agency's campaigns. Consider the cultural and regional nuances that resonate with target audiences.

By staying ahead of these predictions and trends, your digital marketing agency can remain innovative, competitive, and valuable to clients. Embrace these changes as opportunities to deliver exceptional results and meet the evolving needs of the digital landscape.

Emerging Technologies Shaping the Future of Digital Marketing

In this final chapter, we'll explore the fascinating world of emerging technologies that are poised to reshape the future of the digital marketing industry. As technology evolves at an unprecedented pace, staying informed about these innovations is vital for digital marketing agencies to remain at the forefront of the industry.

The Rise of Artificial Intelligence (AI)

The Role of AI: Artificial Intelligence, including machine learning and natural language processing, is revolutionizing digital marketing. AI enhances personalization, automates tasks, and predicts consumer behavior.

Example: Chatbots and Personalization

Augmented Reality (AR) and Virtual Reality (VR)

The Impact of AR and VR: AR and VR technologies offer immersive experiences that captivate audiences. They enable interactive product demonstrations, virtual showrooms, and engaging storytelling.

Example: IKEA's AR Furniture App

Voice Search and Smart Assistants

Voice Technology's Role: Voice search is becoming increasingly prevalent with the rise of smart speakers. Optimizing for voice search is crucial as consumers use voice commands to find information and products.

Example: Voice-Activated Marketing

Blockchain Technology

Blockchain's Impact: Blockchain enhances transparency and security in digital advertising. It can eliminate fraud, ensure ad placement accuracy, and enhance trust in the industry.

Example: AdChain

5G Technology

The Power of 5G: The rollout of 5G networks promises faster internet speeds and reduced latency. This enables real-time experiences, such as high-quality live streaming and AR applications.

Example: Enhanced Live Streaming

Internet of Things (IoT)

IoT in Marketing: The IoT connects devices and gathers data that can inform marketing strategies. Smart devices, wearables, and connected appliances offer new touchpoints for marketers.

Example: Personalized IoT Marketing

Big Data and Predictive Analytics

Harnessing Data: Big data analytics and predictive modeling enable agencies to anticipate consumer behavior, optimize ad spend, and deliver more effective campaigns.

Example: Netflix's Content Recommendations

Quantum Computing (Futuristic Potential)

Quantum Leap: Though in its infancy, quantum computing has the potential to revolutionize data analysis, offering unprecedented processing power for complex tasks like AI training and optimization.

Example: Quantum-Accelerated AI

- In the future, quantum computing may accelerate AI training, leading to more advanced personalization and predictive capabilities.

Emerging Technologies: Future-Proofing Your Agency

As you explore these emerging technologies, consider how they can be integrated into your agency's services. Staying informed and experimenting with these innovations will position your agency as a forward-thinking industry leader, ready to shape the digital marketing landscape of the future.

Conclusion

the Dynamic World of Digital Marketing

Finally we reflect on the journey through the dynamic world of digital marketing. We've explored various aspects of running a successful digital marketing agency, from understanding the fundamentals to scaling your operations and managing multi-channel campaigns. Now, it's time to wrap up our discussion and consider the ongoing quest for excellence in this ever-evolving field.

Reflecting on Your Digital Marketing Journey

As you reach the end of this guide, take a moment to reflect on your own journey in the world of digital marketing. Consider the knowledge and insights you've gained, the strategies you've implemented, and the challenges you've overcome. Reflect on the growth and evolution of your agency.

Real-Life Task: Self-Reflection

Task: Write a brief reflection on your digital marketing journey, highlighting key learnings, achievements, and moments of growth. Consider the following questions:

.

What were the most significant insights or strategies you gained from this guide that had a positive impact on your agency?

.

.

Can you recall a specific challenge or obstacle you faced in your digital marketing journey and how you successfully navigated it?

.

.

How has your agency evolved or grown since you began your digital marketing endeavors? Are there specific milestones or achievements you're proud of?

.

The Ongoing Quest for Excellence

One of the defining characteristics of the digital marketing industry is its continuous evolution. What works today may not work tomorrow, as new technologies, platforms, and consumer behaviors emerge. Therefore, the quest for excellence in digital marketing is ongoing.

Real-Life Task: Continuous Learning Plan

Task: Develop a plan for continuous learning and professional development in the field of digital marketing:

.

Learning Goals: Identify specific areas or topics within digital marketing that you want to deepen your knowledge in. This could include emerging trends, advanced strategies, or specialized skills.

.

.

Learning Resources: Research and compile a list of educational resources, such as online courses, webinars, industry conferences, and books, that align with your learning goals.

.

.

Implementation: Create a schedule or timeline for when you will engage with these resources and allocate time for learning within your agency's operations.

.

.

Application: Identify opportunities to apply what you've learned to your agency's campaigns and strategies. Experiment with new approaches and assess their effectiveness.

.

Real-Life Success Story:

Case Study: Neil Patel's Commitment to Learning

Neil Patel, a renowned digital marketer, has consistently stayed at the forefront of the industry by committing to continuous learning. He dedicates time to experimenting with new marketing techniques, tracking industry trends, and sharing his insights with the community. This commitment has contributed to his enduring success.

As you continue your digital marketing journey, remember that excellence is a pursuit, not a destination. Embrace change, stay curious, and adapt to the evolving landscape of digital marketing.

Leaving a Legacy of Digital Marketing Excellence

Finally, consider the legacy you want to leave in the world of digital marketing. What impact do you want your agency to have? How do you envision contributing to the growth and innovation of the industry?

Real-Life Task: Legacy Statement

Task: Write a legacy statement for your agency—a concise statement that captures the enduring impact you aspire to make in digital marketing. Consider the following elements:

.

Purpose: What is the overarching purpose or mission of your agency in the digital marketing landscape?

.

.

Values: What values or principles will guide your agency's actions and decisions as it continues to evolve?

.

.

Impact: How do you envision your agency contributing to the growth and excellence of the digital marketing industry?

.

Example Legacy Statement:

"At [Your Agency Name], we are dedicated to pioneering innovative digital marketing strategies that not only drive results for our clients but also inspire positive change within the industry. Our commitment to transparency, creativity, and client success will be our lasting legacy, setting new standards for excellence in digital marketing."

In crafting your legacy statement, you articulate your agency's vision for the future and the impact you intend to make on the dynamic world of digital marketing.

As we conclude this guide, remember that the world of digital marketing is boundless in its potential. Embrace the challenges, seize the opportunities, and continue your journey with the spirit of exploration and a commitment to excellence. Your agency's success and impact in this dynamic field are limited only by your imagination and determination.

Thank you for joining us on this journey through the ever-evolving world of digital marketing. We wish you continued success and innovation in your endeavors.

Appendices:

Appendix A: Digital Marketing Resources Appendix B: Recommended Tools and Software Appendix C: Glossary of Digital Marketing Terms Appendix D: Sample Digital Marketing Reports and Templates Appendix E: Additional Reading and References

Acknowledgments:

We extend our heartfelt gratitude to the digital marketing community, our clients, colleagues, and mentors who have contributed to our collective knowledge and inspired our pursuit of excellence in this dynamic field. Your insights, experiences, and dedication to innovation have been invaluable.

Thank you for embarking on this digital marketing journey

with us. We hope you find continued inspiration and success in the dynamic world of digital marketing.

The Ultimate Guide to Digital Marketing Agency

Author: Megbo Beauty

PRAISE FOR AUTHOR

Index

This index provides a concise reference to the content in your table of contents.

www.ingramcontent.com/pod-product-compliance
Lightning Source LLC
LaVergne TN
LVHW051333050326
832903LV00031B/3504